"Dr. Joseph L. White, the Father... mate scholar, teacher, educator, a... tion of his 'Freedom Train'; a tra... of generations of his mentees who continue to carry his legacy of examining the effects of the lack of cultural representation in mental health, educational research, and organizational leadership, forward. Joe (as he was affectionately known to all) always said he would know it was time for him to rest when his mentees surpassed him – this book is a testimony to everything he poured into those who have contributed their outstanding work to this book."

The White Sisters (Lori White, Lynn White Kell, and Lisa White)

"By reading the chapters in this text, you will bear witness to Dr. White's enduring contribution to the lives of past and future generations. The futures of (liberation) psychologies are bright because of the paths Dr. White paved. Hop on the Freedom Train. Be inspired to continue the legacy of Dr. White."

Helen A. Neville, *Professor of Educational Psychology and African American Studies, University of Illinois Urbana-Champaign*

Practical Social Justice

Practical Social Justice brings together the mentorship experiences of a diverse group of leaders across business, academia, and the public sector. They relay the lessons they learned from Dr. Joseph L. White through personal narratives, providing a critical analysis of their experience, and share their best practices and recommendations for those who want to truly live up to their potential as leaders and mentors.

As one of the founding members of the Association of Black Psychologists, the Equal Opportunity Program, and the "Freedom Train," this book focuses on celebrating Dr. White's legacy, and translating real-world experience in promoting social justice change. Experiential narratives from contributors offer a framework for both the mentee and the mentor, and readers will learn how to develop people and infrastructure strategically to build a sustainable legacy of social justice change. They will be presented with ways to pragmatically focus on social justice efforts, favoring results over ego. This is a unique and highly accessible book that will be useful across disciplines and generations, in which the authors illustrate how to build relationships, inspire buy-in, and develop mutually beneficial partnerships that move people and systems toward a more equitable, inclusive, and just future. Providing a personal guide to developing an infrastructure for institutional change, *Practical Social Justice* is based on over half a century of triumph, translated through the lenses of leaders who have used these lessons to measurable and repeatable success.

This book will be essential reading for undergraduate and graduate students in the fields of Psychology, Social Work, Ethnic Studies, Sociology, Public Policy, Leadership, Communications, Business, and Educational Administration. It is also important reading for professionals including leaders and policy makers in organizations dealing with issues around diversity, equity, and inclusion, and anyone interested in promoting social justice.

Bedford Palmer II, Ph.D., is Associate Professor of Counseling at Saint Mary's College of California, USA, and a licensed psychologist. He focuses his work on issues of social justice and multiculturalism. He produced and co-hosted the *Naming It* podcast and is the author of the *Healthy Conversation* children's book series.

Practical Social Justice

Diversity, Equity, and Inclusion
Strategies Based on the Legacy of
Dr. Joseph L. White

Edited by Bedford Palmer II

Routledge
Taylor & Francis Group

NEW YORK AND LONDON

Cover image: Copyright © Getty Images

First published 2023
by Routledge
605 Third Avenue, New York, NY 10158

and by Routledge
4 Park Square, Milton Park, Abingdon, Oxon, OX14 4RN

Routledge is an imprint of the Taylor & Francis Group, an informa business

© 2023 selection and editorial matter, Bedford Palmer II;
individual chapters, the contributors

ISBN: 978-0-367-67803-6 (hbk)
ISBN: 978-0-367-65411-5 (pbk)
ISBN: 978-1-003-13289-9 (ebk)

DOI: 10.4324/9781003132899

Typeset in Times New Roman
by codeMantra

This book is about the work of Dr. Joseph L. White and his impact on his mentees. If you ever had the pleasure of meeting Dr. White, he would likely have taken whatever moments you shared to help you progress in your education, career, or life. If you were moved to thank him after this, he would have told you that it was unnecessary. Instead, he would have charged you to use whatever you gained to pay the blessing forward and help four people who needed it. With that in mind, I dedicate this book to those four more people and all the people who were not blessed to have the opportunity to meet Joe. If this book somehow helps you, please use those gifts and take the time to help four mentees of your own.

Contents

Foreword

All aboard! The Freedom Train is now departing. Join the journey, be part of the experience.

Initially established to connect underrepresented (mostly Black) undergraduate students to graduate programs in clinical psychology, Dr. Joseph White worked hard through the decades to expand the railways of the Freedom Train, inviting engineers and conductors to help build the vision. The metaphorical train consists of interrelated networks and communities committed to the development of Black, Indigenous, and other People of Color psychologists; the journey is as important as the destination, that is, the journey toward personal empowerment and freedom and transformation of the discipline. In the spirit of collectivity, Dr. White reinforced the responsibility for those who have been on the journey longer to assist newer travelers.

No single person has touched the lives of generations of Black, Indigenous, and other People of Color psychologists and trainees more than Dr. White. For half a century, Dr. White mentored countless students and early career and seasoned professionals. He is one of the few people whose mentorship spanned professional identity, as he provided sage advice and support to people working in applied settings and academia. Moreover, he helped leaders create more racially and ethnically diverse psychology and mental health settings and work toward incorporating more culturally resonate and humanizing paradigms, or what we now widely refer to as decolonizing the training.

I met Dr. Joseph White around 1994 when I was an assistant professor at the University of Missouri-Columbia. This was the first of many times I heard him present. Like everyone in attendance, I was enraptured by his brilliant lecture. He pulled the audience into the narrative with his wit and storytelling prowess. People stayed for the engaging synthesis of research and practice on his emerging work with Michael E. Connor on Black fathers. Dr. White had a knack for taking complex phenomena and distilling them into digestible units. In fact, he championed the importance of disseminating research findings in a practical way to a broad range of audiences. His presentations were thus accessible to community members, students, applied psychologists, and faculty alike. And this talk was no exception.

As one could imagine, having individual time with the godfather of Black Psychology as a junior scholar in counseling psychology and Black Studies was a dream come true. I treasured my intimate conversation with Dr. White during this first campus visit. He asked questions about who I was as a person and inquired about my graduate training experiences and my research. He shared with me the history of the Association of Black Psychology and stories about academia. What surprised me more than anything is that years after our initial discussion, he referenced content from this first meeting whenever I saw him. To have someone of Dr. White's stature notice me as an early career professional was validating. He made me feel as though I belonged, even though the academy often negated me as a Black woman and as a Black woman studying the experiences of Black people and naming racism in my scholarship.

As I reflect on my nearly 30-year career, the influence of Dr. White on my professional development looms large. He paved the pathway for me to understand my worth as a human being and as a scholar; he nurtured my intellectual curiosity, and he role modeled cultural humility as a professional and the power of mentoring. Throughout my journey, I often reflect on his affirmation, "Do not look for validation from those who oppress you." This became my mantra going up for tenure. As you will read in the powerful stories in this collection, this statement – or what I like to refer to as a Dr. White proverb – helped many. This concise teaching encouraged me to turn to like-minded scholars and the community for validation and constructive critique of my work. And the words gave me permission to divest in the pursuit of white appeasement.

Like the psychologists whose testimonies you will read in the following pages, I am the professional I am today because of Dr. White. I say this not only because of his personal influence on me but also because of his contributions to shaping a new discipline from a transformative, liberatory lens. Without Dr. White, we do not have Black Psychology, with its strengths-based and freedom-focused core. Drawing on collective wisdom, Dr. White authored *Toward a Black Psychology*, which he intentionally published in the popular *Ebony* magazine. He wanted to first introduce this new framework to those who would be most impacted by this emerging discipline. In the article, he outlined the premise of many liberation psychologies: that a people have the right to self-definition. Rejecting the deficit models in Western psychology, Dr. White argued that a Black Psychology (a) is *strengths-based*, (b) *represents the voices of the people* rather than the voices of those in the ivory tower, (c) *belongs to the people* which is necessary to empower individuals and communities toward wellness and self-determination, and (d) is *written in an understandable manner* (White, 1970).

As the chapters in this book outline, Dr. White's visionary leadership contributed to the development of individuals, institutions, and disciplines (e.g., Black Psychology, Western psychology, multicultural psychology). His foundational text, *The Psychology of Blacks: An Afro-American Perspective* (White & Parham, 1984; White & Parham, 1990), was assigned in classrooms across the country. I know I relied heavily on his writing when I developed and taught the African American Psychology course at the University of Missouri.

Dr. White pioneered liberation and social justice mentoring through his practice. Even before conceptual frameworks describing social justice mentoring, Dr. White created transformative spaces for people to harness their potential. Through the Freedom Train, he fostered mentoring networks, provided meaningful learning and training opportunities, and promoted intergenerational communities among Black, Indigenous, and People of Color psychology professionals. Dr. White maintained long-term mentoring relationships which were mutually beneficial and based on dignity and shared humanity. He instilled hope in others as they did the inward and outward work needed for liberation. By reading the chapters in this text, you will bear witness to Dr. White's enduring contribution to the lives of past and future generations. The futures of (liberation) psychologies are bright because of the paths Dr. White paved.

Hop on the Freedom Train. Be inspired to continue the legacy of Dr. White.

Helen A. Neville

References

White, J. (1970). Toward a Black Psychology. *Ebony*, *25*(11), 44–45.

White, J. L., Parham, T. A. (1984). *The Psychology of Blacks: An Afro-American Perspective*. Englewood Cliffs, NJ: Prentice Hall.

White, J. L., Parham, T. A. (1990). *The Psychology of Blacks: An Afro-American Perspective* (2nd ed.). Englewood Cliffs, NJ: Prentice Hall.

Preface

"You can find me at the top of the Marriott," I remember Dr. White saying to a group of my peers and me as he walked from one presentation to the next. I was a graduate student attending the American Psychological Association (APA) annual convention, which was being held in San Francisco. As one of Dr. White's mentees, I knew that his quick statement was an invitation for us to all meet him in the restaurant bar that occupied the top floor of his favorite hotel in the city. I also knew that when I joined the cross-generational group of mentees and colleagues, I would be swept up in the impromptu networking event that Dr. White called "the Set."

Whether at the top of the Marriott in San Francisco or the lobby bar in another city, walking into the Set was a heady yet predictable experience. Invariably you would come upon a group of people who have pulled all the chairs and tables together (without asking permission) with Dr. White somewhere in the center. As one of Dr. White's mentees who had already been to many Sets in the past, I would usually walk in with a group of new people in tow. Dr. White would say, "Bedford Palmer! The future of Black psychology!" "Go over to the bar, get me a glass of pinot noir, get yourself a drink, and tell your folks that they can order whatever they want."

After following these instructions, Dr. White would check in with me about how I was doing in my program, and then he would have me or another mentee relate one of Dr. White's stories. We would tell the group about him telling us about his exploits, or more likely, we would tell a story about how we accomplished something based on Dr. White's advice or intervention. As the night moved forward, I would watch as Dr. White interacted with each of the people in attendance, checking in as he had with me. At some point, he would call me over to talk to the person he was currently sitting with as he got up to speak to the next. Dr. White would let me know how I and my fellow mentee overlapped and what I should help them with. Then he would be off to the next mentee while I provided whatever insight I could to my fellow mentee.

After Dr. White transitioned and joined the ancestors, I sat in the hotel bar with a group of his mentees during the first APA convention that any of us attended without him in the world. I remember the shared feelings of sadness and nostalgia. We talked about our experiences with Dr. White, and we tried to be helpful and supportive of each other in the way that he would have expected. But I could not shake the deep sense of loss. Both Dr. White as a man, a mentor, and for me, the only grandfather figure I really knew; and for the magic of the Set and how it felt to be part of his Freedom Train that just kept chugging along, sweeping new people on board.

The inspiration for this book was born in the need to offset that feeling of loss. I hoped to bring a group of Dr. White's mentees together to share the experience of one aspect of Dr. White's life work. This is not a biography, as I am not a historian. Instead, it is a blueprint for anyone who cares to read it. Dr. White's work was a clinic on how to demand social justice and make practical gains. If, as Dr. Martin Luther King Jr. said, "the arc of the moral universe is long but it bends toward justice," then Dr. White was pushing on one of the levers.

Dr. Joseph L. White was one of the first Black psychologists in the United States. He was a founding member of the Association of Black Psychologists and the founder of the Equal Opportunity Program, a California statewide educational support program for first-generation, low-income, and minority students. Dr. White was also pivotal in developing the first Ethnic Studies Program at San Francisco State University, which initiated the national ethnic studies movement. Dr. White demonstrated an unwavering commitment to two major themes throughout his career. The first was to change the systems and institutions he interacted with, making them more inclusive and socially just. Dr. White was a master of developing transformative systems that fostered these changes on the local, regional, and national levels. The second theme was to nurture the potential of students from marginalized communities. He accomplished this using a strength-based model of narrative learning, multi-level mentorship, and the active cultivation of professional and academic opportunities for the growth and development of his mentees. All of this was facilitated via a network of friends, colleagues, former and current students, and through the development of several pipelines across academia, government, and corporate America. These two themes came together to embody Dr. White's impact on the field of psychology, the world of academia, and the browning of society.

Practical Social Justice is focused on translating real-world experience into promoting social justice change on the personal and institutional level. More specifically, my goal was to develop a resource that uses the narratives of Dr. White's mentees to provide an experiential understanding of participation in the Freedom Train, as well as provide critical reflections from its riders and conductors, and examples of best practices for overcoming barriers to diversity, inclusion, and equity within academic, governmental, and corporate settings.

This book will be centered on the personal narratives of social justice change-makers, who share the experience of being mentored or otherwise influenced by Dr. Joseph L. White and his generations of mentees. The contributing authors will provide best practices and recommendations for individuals seeking to make substantive change, not only in terms of the specific institution they are engaged with but also over the course of their careers. Through our experiences, we deliver a personal guide to developing an infrastructure for institutional change based on over half a century of triumph, translated through the practical lenses of leaders who have used these lessons to measurable and repeatable success.

You will learn strategies for building a legacy of social justice change through the development of people and infrastructure that will continue outside of your direct efforts. You will be presented with a pragmatic approach to change, which is more focused on socially just results than performative and ego-based stances. This book will be useful across disciplines and generations, as the lessons that we present will be focused on building relationships, developing buy-in, and engaging in a mutually beneficial collaboration that moves people and systems into an inevitably more diverse and equitable future.

This book consists of four sections divided into 12 chapters, each themed with a quote from Dr. White. In Section I (*Keep the Faith*), the authors provide insight into developing social justice advocates, providing practical strategies for mentorship, supporting students, developing professionals, and developing intersectional allyship relationships. In Section II (*Making Something from Nothing*), authors offer examples of paradigm changes in systems, describing engagement with activism and development as activists, shaping more significant concepts like cultural psychology and multicultural competence, and using pipelines to change the demographics of established institutions. The chapters in Section III (*Getting Strong in the Broken Places*) consist of insights into approaches to institutional change. The authors explain how to develop systemic change, describing their experiences in relation to developing culturally specific professional organizations, and how to impact policy decisions at a local and national level. The book will close with Section IV (*Don't Look for Validation in the Faces of Your Oppressor*), where authors describe strategies for navigating oppressive spaces; developing an essential voice within organizations; positioning oneself, colleagues, and mentees for success; and developing influence from the margins.

Each chapter consists of four subsections. The first is a first-person narrative focused on an interaction or series of interactions with Dr. Joseph L. White. The second subsection of each chapter consists of an analysis of the authors' first-person narrative, providing insight into the focus of the chapter. The third subsection of each chapter is a list of practical strategies for addressing the topics discussed in the analysis section. Finally, the authors provide a list of discussion questions to help you better integrate the narrative, analysis, and practical strategies sections; and relate those lessons to your personal circumstances. This structure is meant to simulate the experience of being part of the Set. Imagine each chapter as you being ushered by Dr. White to sit with his mentee(s) so that they can share what they learned from him and they can share their practical expertise. Welcome to the Freedom Train.

Bedford Palmer II

Acknowledgment

I want to express my thanks and respect to all the people who assisted in producing this book. First, I want to express my love and gratitude to my wife, Jenée Scott Palmer. Thank you for giving me the space to dedicate so much time to this book in the face of a global pandemic, lockdowns, wildfires, and a number of significant personal losses. Thank you for the supportive words, the active listening, the reminders to eat, and the times when you told me to put the computer away and just rest. Next, I would like to thank Dr. Nita Tewari for setting me up with her publisher and mentoring me through this process. I am also grateful to my publisher Eleanor Taylor from Routledge for believing in this project from the start and walking with me through the process. Next, thank you to the White family, Lori, Lynn, Lisa, and Lois, for supporting my sharing of Dr. White's work. Finally, I want to express my deepest gratitude to the contributing authors who gave their time and genius to make this book a reality.

Contributors

Editor

Bedford Palmer II, Ph.D., is Associate Professor and Chair of the Counseling Department at Saint Mary's College of California, USA.

Contributors

Hector Y. Adames, Psy.D., is Assistant Professor of Clinical Psychology at the Chicago School of Professional Psychology, USA.

Adisa T. Anderson, Ph.D., is Assistant Director/Manager at UC Berkeley's Counseling and Psychological Services, USA.

Taisha Caldwell-Harvey, Ph.D., is a licensed psychologist and the founder and CEO of The Black Girl Doctor, a mental health practice specializing in therapy, coaching, and workplace wellness for Black women.

Jeanett Castellanos, Ph.D., is Professor of Teaching and Associate Dean of Undergraduate Studies in the School of Social Sciences at the University of California, Irvine, USA.

Anne Chan, Ph.D., is a diversity/mentoring consultant and a licensed psychotherapist in the San Francisco Bay Area, USA. She is the author of *Inspire, Empower, Connect: Reaching across Cultural Differences to Make a Real Difference.*

Nayeli Y. Chavez-Dueñas, Ph.D., is Professor of Counseling Psychology in the Chicago School of Professional Psychology, USA.

Le Ondra Clark Harvey, Ph.D., is Chief Executive Officer at the California Council of Community Behavioral Health Agencies (CBHA) and Executive Director of the California Access Coalition, USA.

Kevin Cokley, Ph.D., is Professor of African and African Diaspora Studies at the University of Texas at Austin, USA.

Michael E. Connor, Ph.D., is Emeritus Professor in the Psychology Department at California State University, Long Beach, USA.

Veronica Franco, M.S., is a doctoral candidate in the combined Counselling, Clinical, and School Psychology program at the University of California, Santa Barbara, USA.

Jerell B. Hill, Ed.D., is Dean of the School of Human Development and Education at Pacific Oaks College, USA.

Jennifer L. Lovell, Ph.D., is Associate Professor of Clinical Psychology at California State University, Monterey Bay, USA.

Helen A. Neville, Ph.D., is Professor of Educational Psychology and African American Studies at the University of Illinois at Urbana-Champaign, USA.

Gerald Parham is Director of Camp Program Development for the Department of Intercollegiate Athletics at the University of California, Irvine, USA.

Thomas A. Parham, Ph.D., is the 11th president of California State University, Dominguez Hills (CSUDH), USA.

William D. Parham, Ph.D., ABPP, is Professor in the Counseling Program, School of Education at Loyola Marymount University, and Director of the Mental Health and Wellness Program of the National Basketball Players Association, USA.

Randi E. Scott-McLaughlin, Ph.D., is Advanced Fellow in Mental Illness Research and Treatment at VISN 2 Mental Illness Research, Education, and Clinical Center (MIRECC), James J. Peters VA Medical Center, New York, USA.

Nita Tewari, Ph.D., is a consultant for mental health, diversity, and South Asian Americans and founder of The SPACE Lab focused on digital mental health and social media impression management.

Section I

Developing Social Justice Advocates – "Keep the Faith"

1 Finding Power

Dr. White's Social Justice Mentoring

Anne Chan

Figure 1.1 Image of Joseph L. White and Anne Chan. Provided by and used with permission of Anne Chan (2022).

First-Person Narrative

Dr. White's first assignment for me was to attend a Division 45 awards ceremony at the American Psychological Association (APA) convention. Prior to meeting him, I would have avoided an awards ceremony at all costs, thinking it would be a compilation of boring speeches. Perhaps the deeper truth was that I didn't feel that I belonged in the leagues of the accomplished glitterati. Before the ceremony was over, Dr. White beckoned to me with the words, "C'mon – follow me." Without further explanation, he casually walked up the stage as if he were taking a Sunday stroll in his neighborhood. "What in the world is he doing?" I puzzled, as I reluctantly followed, my hands clammy. I wished that a giant hole

DOI: 10.4324/9781003132899-2

would suddenly appear and swallow me up. Right in front of the cheering crowd, Dr. White then proceeded to introduce me to the man who had just been lauded with the Division 45 Distinguished Career Award five seconds ago.

After the ceremony, Dr. White invited me to join him for lunch. I was quaking with shyness when I arrived and saw that dinner meant sharing food with him and his entourage of 20, all intimidatingly garbed in professional attire. Once again, he introduced me to everyone at the table, from new graduate students like me to senior psychologists who were deans at their universities. At one point, the president of APA stopped by his table. They shook hands like one world dignitary paying tribute to another. Dr. White proceeded to introduce this renowned psychologist to everyone at the table. I had not started even one day of graduate school, and already he had introduced me to the president of APA as if we were on equal footing. His actions that day sent me a crystal clear message: "You belong at this table. You are one of us. You are part of the family."

My relationship with Dr. White spanned 16 years, from the time I was introduced to him to his passing in 2017. Throughout this time, Dr. White and I rarely met in person. At most, we would only see each other twice a year at conferences. But between conferences, he would be in regular contact via phone calls, emails, and letters. Because we had weekly contact, he became my go-to person whenever I ran into any difficulty in graduate school (which was fairly regularly). At the outset of our relationship, he provided his home number, office number, and email. Later on in our relationship, he gave me his cell number when he finally adopted what he called the "White man's tricknology." There was no dragon assistant guarding his entry way – instead Edna, his longtime secretary, and a fount of kindness, would magically get us connected, even if Dr. White were on a business trip three time zones away.

In my first year of graduate school, he called me every Sunday evening with the regularity of a Swiss timepiece. He didn't just say, "Call me when you need me," and leave it at that. Instead, he made the effort to initiate these calls every single Sunday. Every call began with his cheery, "How ya doin' Sister Chan?" When I poured out my Woe of the Week, he would always express sympathy and understanding in his inimitable way ("Ya gotta watch out for the Man, yeah!"). But he never allowed me to get mired in self-pity and hopelessness. Instead, he would talk me off the ledge with a combination of good-natured humor, no-nonsense advice, and nudges to utilize the resources that he had provided for me. "Ya just gotta make somethin' out of nothin'!" he would encourage me, not letting me get trapped in a deficit mindset.[1] He was well aware of issues of privilege, racism, and inequity but always steered me in a forward momentum while providing resources to shore me up. He pinpointed the conferences that I should attend, ranging from the gigantic APA to smaller, ethnic-friendly conferences where I could see people who looked like me and who shared my research interests. Dr. White did not stop at telling me about conferences to attend. He would say casually, "If you need help getting to the conference, call Edna. She'll hook you up." This was his way of telling me that he would help me financially to get to the conferences.

Our calls felt like family chats – he shared tidbits of himself and others in the psychology community, like news about the achievements of other mentees as well as his daughters. In between phone calls, he would send psychology books, pamphlets, and articles. I treasured these surprise gifts carefully wrapped in thick envelopes with his Irvine address. I also loved receiving his emails with his signature sign-off "Keep the Faith." Another precious gift that he gave me was the chance to watch him in action when he did his consulting work. He would have me tag along as his "teaching assistant," a role through which he gave me the gift of an insider's look into how a professional and an activist operates on different career platforms. He was always consummately prepared for his speaking engagements, captivating his audience with his intellect, and regaling them with his wit. Although he had handwritten notes, I never once saw him glance at them during his presentations. It was clear he had done his homework beforehand to be able to deliver with such ease and aplomb.

Even though I thought of him as the mentor exemplar, Dr. White was always quick to disabuse me of my notion that he knew everything I needed to know. He was well aware of what support he could or could not provide and encouraged me to seek out other mentors. He made sure that I was introduced to other mentors who had skill sets that were different from his. For instance, one early introduction to an Asian American researcher led to her serving as an invaluable resource and support when I wrote my dissertation.

Throughout our entire relationship, we had an open, respectful, and safe channel of communication. I trusted implicitly that he had my back and that I could go to him with any problem and receive firm support and astute advice in return. He never asked for anything in return, but he did have an unspoken expectation that I would "pass it on." I would like to believe that he came to see me as someone he could count on to support others. Unlike other relationships or friendships that ebb and fade away, I always felt certain that my mentoring relationship with Dr. White would only end when one of us departed this planet.

Analysis of Narrative

For many, social justice might connote sweeping systemic change involving societal, political, legal, educational, and institutional transformation. Dr. White's social justice work certainly targeted these macro levels. Just one example was his tireless championing of the Educational Opportunity Program (EOP), a program that has subsequently made it possible for thousands of historically underprivileged students to attend college in California. At the other end of the spectrum, Dr. White also paid attention to the micro level of individual transformation through his personal outreach and mentoring of students. His mentoring work at this micro level was roundly criticized by naysayers who felt he should have focused his energies on larger systemic forces (J. White, personal communication, July 6, 2016).[2] However, he clearly discerned the connection between mentoring the individual and creating social justice change:

> Back in 1968 ... we wanted to change psychology and we first tried to change psychology by confrontation. And that was part of the evolutionary process. Then it dawned on me that one of the ways to change psychology was to get more talented people into it, and that I was a part of many of those people at one stage or another of their lives, and then they're creating this change ... an organizational change and a change in the epistemology of knowledge because we're saying that there are other foundations of knowledge broader than the ones developed by the experimental, so called "scientific" psychology model.
>
> (J. White, personal communication, March 4, 2004)

Dr. White's words show that he was reconceptualizing and revolutionizing the very way a revolution happens. Instead of focusing solely on the macro level, he rethought the means for creating a revolution by devoting part of his energies on developing individuals who could find their power and band together to create systematic, epistemological, and radical change. His vision was not understood by his critics who excoriated him for mentoring for the benefit of select individuals. But Dr. White had the big picture vision of mentoring for social justice and radical change. He saw that the pipeline problem in higher education is not just a simple infrastructure problem that could be solved with one quick build. He knew that every phase of the pipeline demanded constant maintenance and oversight because each person constituting the pipeline needed help and support from the outset throughout their careers. To address this need, he invested time and effort into supporting each individual comprising each nut and bolt of the pipeline. Through his mentoring, he painstakingly contributed to the building and scaffolding of a robust pipeline of diverse, talented people.

By providing quality mentoring to underserved young people, Dr. White exemplified and embodied the dictum that "the personal is the political is the professional" (Milville, 2018, p. 102). He did not just advocate for social justice (Maxwell & Duckworth, 2020). Instead, he lived it, breathed it, embodied it, and mentored for it. His mentoring actions enfolded the personal, political, and professional in the following ways, as demonstrated in his interactions with me.

Building Trust

Trust is at the heart of a genuine mentoring relationship, particularly when cross-racial and cross-cultural differences are at stake (Chan, 2018; Ream et al., 2014). Without trust, mentees would not feel confidence in their mentors, nor would they feel comfortable confiding and being vulnerable. Developing trust is a particularly sensitive and critical piece in mentoring ethnic minorities who justifiably feel mistrust with authority figures and systems (Chan, 2018). Dr. White did not start any of his mentoring relationships with an expectation that each mentee would automatically trust him. He knew that trust is built over time and that he, the mentor, had to earn the trust of each mentee. He established trust by being willing to give of his time, being easily accessible, and being consistent in his communication. His regular check-ins every Sunday made me feel that he genuinely cared about me. I grew to trust him as a result. My trust in him was also sealed when he told me about himself through his stories (Chan, 2018). He was invariably down-to-earth and approachable, using unpretentious language that told me he was a real person and not some academic artifice. His lack of airs put me at ease in our relationship, thus cementing my trust in him.

Providing Culturally Appropriate Support

Dr. White knew that graduate programs, even those that strive to be multiculturally sensitive, can be spaces where students of color feel invisible, devalued, and demeaned from a plethora of assaults, ranging from microaggressions to overt racist discrimination (Harris & Lee, 2019). He provided culturally appropriate supports as an antidote to these attacks, by introducing his mentees to same-race researchers and pointing them to culturally supportive spaces such as ethnic minority professional organizations (Chan et al., 2015; Delgado-Romero et al., 2012) like the Association of Black Psychologists, the National Latinx Psychological Association, the Asian-American Psychological Association, the Society of Indian Psychologists, and the Division on South Asian Americans. These spaces provided refuge, support, and affirmation for students of color who might not otherwise see themselves or their research interests represented in their faculty.

Providing Resources

In order to be visible in the field, graduate students need to attend and present at national, regional, and local conferences. All of this can add up to a hefty amount when factoring in registration fees, airplane tickets, accommodations, and meals. Graduate students subsisting on their meager university stipends are not usually able to afford such expenditures.

Dr. White would often pay for these expenses so that his mentees got visibility and opportunities. He knew that it was in these conferences where introductions are made, professional relationships are created, and opportunities are revealed. Since most students would not be able to afford going to these conferences, he made it possible for them to go by providing practical support (Chan, 2008; Mangione et al., 2018), thus ensuring they got to advance their careers. He even bought books and paid for meals for his mentees so that they would not only get fed but would also feel that they belonged at his table. He was also generous in sharing intangible resources, such as his time, his knowledge, and his contacts (Chan, 2008).

Providing Positive Affirmation

He was always on the lookout for potential obstacles blocking his mentees and would help them handle each blockade. He knew that even a small obstruction could completely derail a student's progress, so he made sure that he knew what his mentees were up against. Perhaps the biggest obstacle might be in a student's mind – in particular, students of color might question if they belong in the rarefied atmosphere of academia. Imposter syndrome is a particularly pernicious force in people of color in academia who do not see role models who look like them or come from similar backgrounds (Hutchins & Rainbolt, 2017; Peteet et al., 2015). Dr. White would telegraph messages of his belief and validation in his mentees, by direct means, such as explicitly saying "I believe in you," or by indirect ways, such as introducing them to senior people in the field so that they feel like part of the family (Chan, 2008).

Building Networks

Dr. White was intentional and thorough in introducing his mentees to senior people in the field, as he did when he introduced me to the Division 45 awardee and when he introduced all his mentees to the president of APA (Chan, 2008). These introductions served multiple purposes. First, they expanded people's networks in a much quicker way than would have happened otherwise. By myself, I would not likely have ever gotten to meet the president of APA. Dr. White's introduction made an impossible connection happen in a matter of seconds. These introductions opened the door for his mentees to work with seniors in the field. Second, these introductions sent a powerful message to his mentees – "You are part of the family. You are part of my network" was the unequivocal affirmation given with each introduction. Dr. White knew that mentees did not feel like they belonged at the table (Ek et al., 2010). He made introductions to telegraph the message that not only did they belong, but they were also an organic and important part of the whole. Third, Dr. White's introductions served to enlarge the mentee's social capital (Bourdieu, 1997). Even a first-generation immigrant like me received a boost in social capital, thanks to Dr. White's generosity in sharing his network. While discussions of Bourdieuian social capital tend to focus on the individual, Dr. White had a much larger vision for his mentees' social capital. His introductions were not meant solely for the benefit of the individual – he created a strong net of interconnected, social justice-minded folk who would support each other and upcoming generations and, in working together, enact educational and social change. He called this network "The Freedom Train." His unspoken expectation was that we would help each other as he had helped us ("Pass it on" was a frequent theme in his stories).

Role Modeling

Two gaps in the education of psychologists are training in leadership and role model learning (Mats Ohlin & Brodin, 2013). In particular, there is a lack of social justice leadership support for new psychologists, principals, and administrators (Hayes & Angell, 2020; Jones et al., 2013). Dr. White addressed these gaps in two ways: (1) by explaining how the leadership process works and (2) by serving as a role model in the realms of leadership, higher education, and social activism. His mentoring went beyond the didactic and abstract and included an ex-periential component. He included his mentees in his work by bringing them along to observe him in action so they could see how a consultant works or how a professor teaches in a university classroom (Albright et al., 2017). Getting to see him in action was like an education in so-cial justice because he provided a living example of how to integrate social justice concerns into our formal classroom training (Motulsky et al., 2014). It can be hard to imagine oneself as a social activist at the beginning of one's journey. By letting us observe him, Dr. White made it possible for us to see our futures by allowing us to experience his present. Hands-on learning from his professional work and life history were essential components in the development of my critical conscious-ness (Neville, 2014) and my social justice stance and beliefs (Caldwell & Vera, 2010).

Building Resiliency

Those who choose to work on behalf of social justice need to have strength and resiliency to ward off burnout (Gorski, 2019; Gorski & Chen, 2015). Dr. White's signature sign off was "Keep the Faith" – a phrase he used both personally and professionally, at the end of emails to individuals and at keynote speeches to thousands of attendees. These three simple words, "Keep the Faith," were a beacon to stay strong in the face of adversity and to sustain hope that things will always work out. Dr. White never lost sight of the power of human strength, perseverance, and resilience – a particularly important message for those who take the long, hard, and seemingly endless road of social justice work.

Setting Excellence as a Standard

Dr. White role-modeled excellence in all of his professional endeavors. He may have deadpanned that he was just a "nickel-and-dime" consultant, but his actions made it clear that he took his duties seriously and produced quality work for the people who hired him. He often said, half-jokingly, half-seriously, that he did not want people to think he was "raggedy." The last speech I saw him give was nine months before his death. Though frail and wheelchair-bound, he delivered his speech without notes and earned a standing ovation from the audience. Projecting excellence was a standard that he set for himself and his mentees:

> The two behaviors that I want to project and when I'm acting a fool too, is performance and a high standard of excellence. I don't care if it's Black psychology or whatever – that I did it well and that I was clear. And the other that I was credible, that I followed through on what I said I would do.... So excellence and credibility is what I want them [the mentees] to project.
>
> (J. White, personal communication, 2004)

Dr. White's mentoring was all about uncovering opportunities for his mentees. But he also emphasized the importance of excellence as a means toward opportunity. He wanted his mentees to take pride in their work and produce excellence. His promotion of his mentees was not about wink-wink cronyism but about making it possible for their talent and excellence to be utilized.

Imparting Wisdom

In our conversations, he talked often about his life journey, about his experiences as a Black psychologist at a time when the only Black psychologist he had ever seen was the one who stared back at him in the mirror. He talked about his social justice efforts like creating the EOP, fighting for inclusivity from APA, and envisioning a Black psychology. These stories got me thinking about how social change happens and challenged me to figure out how I could contribute. In imparting his wisdom, he did not say, "Do I as do," but he inspired me and many others to act on behalf of social justice in ways that were right for each of us. His stories were transmissions of wisdom and inspiration, lighting the way for us to create social justice in our own manner.

Practical Strategies and Best Practices

Mentoring relationships, particularly across racial divides, necessitates navigating complex territory with numerous pitfalls (Chan, 2018). Dr. White's lived experience in mentoring gives us critical insights into practical strategies for how to mentor effectively. The following are best practices that we can learn from Dr. White's expertise in mentoring:

- Pay attention to the establishment and maintenance of trust in the relationship. Trust is an absolute essential in any mentoring relationship – without trust, a true relationship does not exist. In an optimal mentoring relationship, the mentee feels sufficient trust in the mentor to turn to them for guidance. Effective mentors like Dr. White build trust through a number of key practices such as self-disclosure, maintaining excellent communication, having a holistic understanding of the mentee, and being open to discussing issues of race and culture (Chan, 2018).
- Self-disclose as appropriate, and discuss your social justice efforts. Telling about yourself and your experiences serves two purposes: (1) revealing who you are to the mentee, thus fostering trust; and (2) imparting wisdom of how things are done and lessons learned.
- Be proactive in communication. *Don't* just wait for mentees to call you. *Do* call them, check on them, and initiate contact.
- Be easily accessible. Make it easy for them to get a hold of you to show them that you truly welcome their presence.
- Be proactive in providing resources, such as books, information to scholarships and grants, and information on career development opportunities.
- Build confidence, resiliency, and a sense of belonging through positive affirmation. Tell your mentees you believe in them and that they belong at the table. Send encouraging messages. Keep them going when they are down.
- Remove or help clear barriers. Blocks to success can occur in any shape, size, or form in a career trajectory, from the individual level (such as interpersonal strife or difficulties with a statistics course) to larger macro levels like the departmental (such as politics between faculty that affect students), university, and societal levels (such as racism and traumatic events like the murder of George Floyd) (Chan et al., 2015). Identify these blocks, and provide options and strategies for mentees when they encounter these roadblocks.
- Create a sense of community through networks. Introduce them to your network, and teach them how to expand their networks. Put thought and effort into helping them get connected to people who can partner with them or further their careers. Take them to conferences, and make personal introductions.

- Show them the nuts and bolts of how things are done and how organizations operate. Take your mentees with you when you are doing professional work so they can see social justice work in action. Have them observe and learn about your professional practice. Go over practical things like how to format a curriculum vitae, create a syllabus, and write a personal statement.
- Know that you cannot do it all alone – have a network of mentors ready to take on different aspects of mentoring.
- Keep the Faith – recognize that working to effect social change can easily lead to burnout. Maintain a spirit of faith and optimism that things will work out, as Dr. White always did when he advised us to "Keep the Faith."

Discussion Questions

1 How much time do I spend with my mentees?
2 How are my actions leading to building trust with my mentee?
3 In what ways am I accessible to my mentee?
4 What is one step I can take to become a better mentor?
5 What are the barriers (individual, departmental/organizational, systemic, societal) facing my mentees and how can I help them overcome these obstacles?
6 What resources do I have that I can share with my mentee?
7 In what ways can I build my mentees' resiliency and hope?
8 How do I model excellence to my mentee?
9 How do I demonstrate that I am keeping the faith?
10 Who are in my network who can support me in my mentoring efforts?
11 In what ways can I improve on being a social justice-minded mentor?

By reaching out and mentoring students of all colors, Dr. White was a change agent in every sense of the word. He had a natural, irreplicable ability to connect with people from diverse backgrounds. Well before the Black Lives Matter movement, he made his mentees feel that their lives mattered. This chapter cannot do justice to the dynamism of Dr. White's mentoring. I can only attempt to distill the elements of his elixir of goodwill. From these basic fundamentals, I would like to encourage people to formulate their own special brand of mentoring and to go forth and mentor. I would like to close this chapter with Dr. White's own words that he said to me in one of our last conversations before he passed: "If a human being can find their own power, it enables them to help others find it" (J. White, personal communication, April 16, 2016). Through mentoring, Dr. White did everything within his power to help others find their power. The 100-plus PhDs he mentored have subsequently gone on to assist upcoming generations, thus redistributing power and making social change happen. He not only leveled the playing field for those from less privileged backgrounds, but he also transformed the field of psychology itself by nurturing talented people of color into leadership positions. Now that Dr. White has passed, it is up to us to preserve his legacy and continue the work that he did. For me, it is providing quality mentoring in the way he mentored me and teaching others about the Dr. White brand of mentoring. Thank you, Dr. White, for all the love you poured into each one of us.

Notes

1 In the educational research literature, deficit models have been utilized by some researchers to explain the achievement gap between White and minority students. These researchers attribute the gap to "deficiencies" in the culture and background of minority students. My deficit mindset – my belief that I was less than qualified and unprepared for graduate school – was unconsciously drawn from these long-standing, racially biased educational theories. Dr. White, on the contrary, lived, breathed, and championed the opposite point of view – that minority students had cultural strengths and values that they could leverage to succeed in academia.
2 From 2004 to 2016, I conducted formal interviews with Dr. White. The quotations from this chapter are from these interviews.

References

Albright, J. N., Hurd, N. M., & Hussain, S. B. (2017). Applying a social justice lens to youth mentoring: A review of the literature and recommendations for practice. *American Journal of Community Psychology, 59*(3–4), 363–381. https://doi.org/10.1002/ajcp.12143

Bourdieu, P. (1997). The forms of capital. In A. H. Halsey, H. Lauder, & P. Brown (Eds.), *Education: Culture, economy, society* (pp. 46–58). Oxford: Oxford University Press.

Caldwell, J. C., & Vera, E. M. (2010). Critical incidents in counseling psychology professionals' and trainees' social justice orientation development. *Training and Education in Professional Psychology, 4*(3), 163–176. https://doi.org/10.1037/a0019093

Chan, A. W. (2008). Mentoring ethnic minority, pre-doctoral students: An analysis of key mentor practices. *Mentoring & Tutoring: Partnership in Learning, 16*(3), 263–277.

Chan, A. (2018). Trust-building in the mentoring of students of color. *Mentoring & Tutoring: Partnership in Learning, 26*(1), 4–29. https://doi.org/10.1080/13611267.2017.1416265

Chan, A. W., Yeh, C. J., & Krumboltz, J. D. (2015). Mentoring ethnic minority counseling and clinical psychology students: A multicultural, ecological, and relational model. *Journal of Counseling Psychology, 62*(4), 592–607. https://doi.org/10.1037/cou0000079

Delgado-Romero, E. A., Forrest, L., & Lau, M. Y. (2012). Ethnic minority psychological associations: Connections to counseling psychology. *The Counseling Psychologist, 40*(5), 630–645. http://doi.org/10.1177/0011000011420173

Ek, L. D., Cerecer, P. D. Q., Alanis, I., & Rodriguez, M. A. (2010). "I don't belong here": Chicanas/Latinas at a Hispanic serving institution creating community through muxerista mentoring. *Equity & Excellence in Education, 43*(4), 539–553. https://doi.org/10.1080/10665684.2010.510069

Gorski, P. C. (2019). Fighting racism, battling burnout: Causes of activist burnout in US racial justice activists. *Ethnic and Racial Studies, 42*(5), 667–687. https://doi.org/10.1080/01419870.2018.1439981

Gorski, P. C. & Chen, C. (2015). "Frayed all over:" The causes and consequences of activist burnout among social justice education activists. *Educational Studies, 51*(5), 385–495. https://doi.org/10.1080/00131946.2015.1075989

Harris, T. M. & Lee, C. N. (2019). Advocate-mentoring: A communicative response to diversity in higher education. *Communication Education, 68*(1), 103–113. https://doi.org/10.1080/03634523.2018.1536272

Hayes, S. D., & Angelle, P. S. (2020). Relational mentoring for supporting school principals in social justice leadership. In C. A. Mullen (Ed.), *Handbook of social justice interventions in education.* Springer. https://doi.org/10.1007/978-3-030-29553-0_98-1

Hutchins, H. M. & Rainbolt, H. (2017). What triggers imposter phenomenon among academic faculty? A critical incident study exploring antecedents, coping, and development opportunities. *Human Resource Development International, 20*(3), 194–214. https://doi.org/10.1080/13678868.2016.1248205

Jones, J. M., Sander, J. B., & Booker, K. W. (2013). Multicultural competency building: Practical solutions for training and evaluating student progress. *Training and Education in Professional Psychology, 7*(1), 12–22. https://doi.org/10.1037/a0030880

Mangione, L., Borden, K. A., Nadkarni, L., Evarts, K., & Hyde, K. (2018). Mentoring in clinical psychology programs: Broadening and deepening. *Training and Education in Professional Psychology, 12*(1), 4–13. https://doi.org/10.1037/tep0000167

Mats Ohlin, J. L., & Brodin, E. M. (2013). Mentorship, supervision and learning experience in PhD education. *Studies in Higher Education, 38*(5), 639–662. https://doi.org/10.1080/03075079.2011.596526

Maxwell, B., & Duckworth, V. (2020). Mentoring as a model of resistance in times of austerity. In C. Woolhouse, & L. Nicholson (Eds.), *Mentoring in higher education.* Palgrave Macmillan. https://doi.org/10.1007/978-3-030-46890-3_15

Milville, M. L. (2018). No rest for the nasty: Mentoring as mobilizing for change and advocacy. *The Counseling Psychologist, 46*(1), 100–115. https://doi.org/10.1177/0011000018754323

Motulsky, S. L., Gere, S. H., Saleem, R., & Trantham, S. M. (2014). Teaching social justice in counseling psychology. *The Counseling Psychologist, 42*(8), 1058–1083. https://doi.org/10.1177/0011000014553855

Neville, H. A. (2014). Social justice mentoring: Supporting the development of future leaders for struggle, resistance, and transformation. *The Counseling Psychologist, 43*(1), 157–169. https://doi.org/10.1177/0011000014564252

Peteet, B. J., Montgomery, L., & Weekes, J. C. (2015). Predictors of imposter phenomenon among talented ethnic minority undergraduate students. *The Journal of Negro Education, 84*(2), 175–186. https://doi.org/10.7709/jnegroeducation.84.2.0175

Ream, R. K., Lewis, J. L., Echeverria, B., & Page, R. N. (2014). Trust matters: Distinction and diversity in undergraduate science education. *Teachers College Record, 116*(5), 1–30. https://www.tcrecord.org/Content.asp?ContentId=17428

2 Creating Community to Support Students of Color

Kevin Cokley

First-Person Narrative

Before I reflect on the lessons that I learned from Dr. White, I need to provide some context for our relationship. While I don't remember the first time I met Dr. White, I do remember the first time I learned about him. It happened when I attended my first academic conference, the American Counseling Association (ACA) conference, in March 1993. I was a master's student in the Counselor Education program at the University of North Carolina at Greensboro, and I had the fortunate opportunity to attend the ACA conference in Atlanta. At the conference, I attended a session by the Association of Multicultural Counseling and Development. I was especially excited to attend the session because Dr. Thomas Parham was the featured speaker. I had become familiar with Dr. Parham in my multicultural counseling class because of my interest in racial identity. During the Q&A, I raised my hand and made a comment. I don't remember what I said, but whatever I said apparently made an impression on Dr. Parham. After the session, Dr. Parham approached me, and I felt like I was in the presence of a celebrity. He was impressed with what I said, and I told him how much I enjoyed being there. He told me that if I thought that conference was good, I should attend the Association of Black Psychologists' (ABPsi) convention. I had never heard of ABPsi, so of course the idea of attending a conference and meeting other famous Black psychologists like Dr. Parham sounded too good to be true. My attitude was basically like, "Where do I sign up?" Then Dr. Parham gave me a signed copy of his book, *The Psychology of Blacks* (White & Parham, 1990). This book would become one of my most prized books. It was also my first academic introduction to Dr. Joseph White.

As previously mentioned, I do not recall the first time I met Dr. White. It most certainly was at an academic conference, most likely the ABPsi conference. What I do clearly remember is that my relationship with Dr. White became closer after I became a professor at Southern Illinois University at Carbondale (SIUC). In 1998, I accepted a tenure track position at SIUC. I was in a new city and new university, and I was a professor in a counseling psychology program that was rich in history. The

DOI: 10.4324/9781003132899-3

program had graduated such luminaries as Thomas Parham, Michael Brown, and Laura Brown and had esteemed professors including Janet Helms, Fredrick Leong, and Tony Tinsley. The counseling psychology program had a long history of graduating students of color, and I was now in a position to help continue that legacy.

Dr. White had established a connection to several universities, including SIUC. I came to understand that he was always looking to cultivate ties to universities as potential places that he could send students to for graduate school. During my early years as an assistant professor, Dr. White would reach out to me and others to arrange for him to visit SIUC and speak. Dr. White was a remarkable speaker who could keep an audience's attention like few speakers I've ever heard. He was a tremendous storyteller, and he had an uncanny ability to make you laugh (often at the same stories) while teaching you valuable lessons. He often told the story about how he and other Black psychologists confronted White psychologists at the American Psychological Association's (APA) 1968 convention about APA's failure to sufficiently address issues impacting Black people.

Dr. White always wanted to let me know when he had students from the University of California at Irvine (UCI) applying. Dr. White was always mentoring and helping students, especially students of color. He wanted to make sure they got accepted in graduate programs where they would be supported and nurtured by faculty who cared for them. I realized that being a professor in SIUC's counseling psychology program came with the added expectation that I would use my position to help facilitate the admission and graduation of students of color. This was all part of what Dr. White referred to as his "Freedom Train," which he established across various universities with the goal of racially and ethnically desegregating and integrating psychology.

A common interaction would look something like this. Dr. White would see me at a conference and motion for me to come over. Often he had a student that he would want to introduce to me. Then, with a gentle squeezing of my arm, he would guide me to an area where he would proceed with the introductions. I should note that while some of these introductions were for a potential future graduate school opportunity, other times it was just Dr. White trying to connect students with professionals that he believed would be good for them to know. Dr. White was tireless in his efforts to connect students with professionals, and he never let an opportunity go wasted where he could facilitate this connection.

In my opinion, one of the many skills that Dr. White had was his ability to see the unlimited potential in students of color as "diamonds in the rough." Dr. White was incredibly perceptive and intuitive. I believe he understood that one of the main reasons psychology did not reflect the diversity of a multicultural America was that there were not enough people in the positions of decision-making during admissions season to look at the whole student and not just having high GPA or GRE scores.

While Dr. White and I never explicitly talked about this, I had the sense that he had the uncanny ability to speak to students, learn about their background and who they were and what their experiences had been, and then determine what schools would be the best fit for them to apply to. I also believe that Dr. White was particularly adept at identifying students of color who may have experienced feelings of self-doubt and the impostor phenomenon and thus needed more support.

The impostor phenomenon has become a focus of much of my research in recent years (Cokley et al., 2013, 2015, 2017). The impostor phenomenon refers to an internal sense of intellectual phoniness that is experienced by individuals who are otherwise smart and accomplished people (Clance & Imes, 1978). During my formative years as a young assistant professor, I was not conducting research on the impostor phenomenon. In fact, I was probably working hard to combat my own impostor feelings trying to make it in the academy! I believe that Dr. White understood that many of the students of color he identified and worked with were talented students full of potential who would greatly benefit from being part of a network of individuals who would support them both personally and professionally. Dr. White understood that the desegregation and integration of psychology would not happen while conducting business as usual. He employed an approach that combined an understanding of Black psychology and multicultural psychology with a family-oriented approach where he sought to make students feel like they were loved and cared for by people invested in their success.

It was always important to Dr. White that he show his mentees, in both word and deed, that he was fully supportive of their professional development. One of the ways he did this was to attend their presentations at academic conferences. Individuals who have ever presented at an academic conference know that it can be an anxiety-provoking experience. This is especially the case for those who have never presented or who have little experience presenting. While it would have been physically impossible for Dr. White to attend every presentation made by all of his mentees, he made what I assume to be calculated decisions about which presentations he would attend. Oftentimes, he would attend the presentations of more novice presenters, typically students, as a show of support for them. In this way, Dr. White was demonstrating that his actions were as important as his words. His presence undoubtedly meant the world to his mentees.

Analysis of Narrative

One of the insights from this narrative is how intentional Dr. White was in connecting people to each other. I especially apply this to myself. Many people were connected to Dr. White because of their affiliation with the UCI. After receiving his Ph.D. from Michigan State University, Dr. White spent most of his career at UCI, where he taught and mentored many students. Many of his students and mentees would go on to become distinguished professionals (e.g., Thomas Parham, Michael Connor, and Horace Mitchell). Even when Dr. White retired from teaching, he never stopped mentoring students and young professionals. At conferences you would frequently see Dr. White surrounded by students, young professionals, as well as mid-career and more seasoned professionals.

For some reason, Dr. White appeared to take a special interest in me, and he was very intentional about trying to always include me in these gatherings. I point this out because I had no connections to UCI. I did not go to school there, and I never worked there. As I previously mentioned, I recall my first interaction with Dr. White being at a conference. While Dr. White had no direct influence on me accepting a position at SIUC, his "star student," Dr. Thomas Parham, had encouraged me to accept the position and provided me advice about negotiating strategies. I suppose one could say that Dr. White's influence on me working at SIUC was indirectly through Dr. Parham.

Reflecting on my narrative about Dr. White leads me to ask the question, "Why did Dr. White take a special interest in me?" For years I tried to answer this question. Our interactions, while significant, were primarily limited to the occasions that I would see him at conferences. It is true that at the first two universities where I taught, Dr. White had significant contacts with individuals whom he had influenced in some way (e.g., Kathleen Chwalisz at SIUC and Laurie Mintz at the University of Missouri at Columbia). I recall those individuals talking very fondly about Dr. White and the work he had done to send students their way. However, it wasn't until I was teaching at the University of Texas at Austin that I was in the position to help bring him as a speaker to the campus.

Even with these memories, I never considered myself to be a formal part of Dr. White's mentor–mentee Freedom Train network. I attribute this to my literal interpretation that to be a part of this network meant that you were either literally one of his students or you were in regular contact with him in an active mentoring relationship. I did not see myself as being in an active mentoring relationship with him, so in my mind, I was not formally a part of the Freedom Train network. In my mind, being a mentor would have meant providing me guidance about publishing (because I was in a publish or perish culture) or the direction that my career should take. I envisioned, perhaps unrealistically, that mentoring would involve providing tangible advice or counsel that would help me excel professionally. While I had a tremendous amount of respect and admiration for Dr. White, this was not the way I had understood or experienced our relationship.

In 2016, the *APA Monitor* published an interview with Dr. White where he reflected on his 60-year career as the "godfather of Black psychology" championing the rights of Black people. He also reflected on his 1968 confrontation with the APA Board of Directors (Angelis, 2016). I read the article with great interest. While I was already familiar with some of the information shared, there were certain details about his personal and professional life that I was not familiar with (e.g., being in graduate school at the same time Malcolm X's brother, Robert Little, was a graduate student in social work at Michigan State; being drawn to psychology by Pavlovian conditioning and Freud's defense mechanisms). When I got to the end of the article, I was stunned to see that included in Dr. White's shortlist of mentees was my name! I thought to myself, "How can this be?" All this time, I never thought of myself as being one of his mentees, and it took me reading this interview to finally understand how Dr. White saw me.

At the time, it was not apparent to me why my name was on the list. Names such as Thomas Parham and Michael Connors were his former students, while other names such as Horace Mitchell and Jeanne Manese were people who worked at their longtime employer, UCI. As I reflect on those interactions through the years, I now understand why my name was on the list. Dr. White had, in his own way, been engaging in a type of loosely structured, informal mentoring with me. I see examples where this informal mentoring is evident. His concern for helping and mentoring students of color was a deeply held professional value that he modeled for me. I believe he saw in me someone who also valued supporting students of color. I think he was showing me that students of color needed people like me who were in faculty positions to advocate for, mentor, and nurture them. No matter how successful I may become, it would mean little if I did not use my position to create opportunities for other students of color. As the adage goes, to whom much is given, much is required. Dr. White was showing me that even in retirement and with all of his impressive professional accomplishments (e.g., being the first Black graduate student in clinical psychology at Michigan State University; being one of the founders of the ABPsi; establishing the Educational Outreach Program at California State University at Long Beach, which became a program implemented across the California State University campuses; serving as Robert Kennedy's campaign director; and serving as a consultant for school districts, universities, and private organizations), he never abdicated his mentoring and support of students of color.

Dr. White's ability to see the unlimited potential in students of color as "diamonds in the rough" is a model for how those of us who are in faculty positions should approach the admission process involving students of color. In fact, it reminds me of my own story applying to graduate school. I was always a "smart" student (or this was how I saw myself) in my K-12 years of school. When I got to college, I experienced a rude awakening and did very poorly in my first semester. Much of my time in college was marked by academic struggle and mediocrity. While deep down I believed that I was a smart person, my grades did not reflect this, and consequently, my academic self-concept took a beating. I was that student whom Dr. White would have seen as a diamond in the rough.

I needed someone to take a chance and give me an opportunity to go to graduate school.

Observing how perceptive and intuitive Dr. White was in identifying students who were diamonds in the rough, and not necessarily straight "A" students or academic superstars, was an incredibly important observation that I made. Dr. White seemed to be instinctually drawn to these individuals. How he was able to do this remains somewhat of a mystery to me. Perhaps it was his clinical instincts as a clinical psychologist. Or maybe it was just the wisdom of having interacted with thousands of students over the years. Whatever the case, Dr. White's ability to identify individuals who could benefit from extra support was absolutely masterful.

When Dr. White attended conference presentations by his mentees, I observed how he would position himself where his mentees could see him. His nonverbal behavior (e.g., nodding his head, making eye contact) was reassuring. He sat like a proud papa who was basking in the presence of his mentees. As I reflect on his behavior, I am reminded of all the presentations that I have given, especially when I was a student and young professional. Like most presenters, I was always concerned about having people attend my presentations. Few things hurt a budding professional more than to put in a lot of time for a presentation only to end up speaking to a room with few people (or in a worst-case scenario, empty room!). I can recall the feelings of disappointment I experienced when my presentations were poorly attended. To have Dr. White attend your presentation was even more impactful given his stature and popularity. Dr. White was a larger-than-life figure, so him making the decision to attend your presentation made you feel special. Dr. White understood this very well. While I did not actively process this lesson at the time, in retrospect I can see how this has likely influenced my own behaviors with my students and mentees (as well as other students whom I try to support).

Practical Strategies

Creating a sense of community is important for all college students. Indeed, you can see various strategies employed by colleges to make students feel a strong sense of attachment and belonging. One of the best examples of this can be seen at Texas A&M University, which has been described as having the most fanatical loyalty any college has ever had (Scherer, 2020). From the moment students step on campus, they are socialized with time-confirmed traditions such as the Corps of Cadets, Aggie Ring, Aggie Code of Honor, and the Aggie Yell, which serve to create a strong sense of loyalty and community among all students. However, it is also true that creating a sense of community is often different for students of color. One student of color at Texas A&M commented that it was at A&M where she first experienced what it was like to be judged first and foremost on the basis of her gender or racial identity (Scherer, 2020).

During the course of my 23 years of teaching, I have engaged in practical strategies that have helped to create a special sense of community for the students of color I have worked with. I should point out that these strategies can be applied to all students regardless of their race, ethnicity, or culture. That said, I believe the strategies are particularly salient for students of color because they often struggle with a sense of belonging in predominantly White educational environments.

Creating a Family Environment

The first and perhaps most important strategy I use is to create a family environment. Beyond biological definitions, a family can be considered to be a group of people who support each other, have each other's back, and have a sense of loyalty, selflessness, love, and genuine care and concern for each other. When I was a young assistant professor at SIUC, I had just moved from Atlanta, a city that many refer to as a Black Mecca because many African American singles, professionals, and middle-class families were drawn to live there. For Black people, there was a level of familiarity and comfort living in Atlanta because Black folks were literally everywhere. Moving to Carbondale, Illinois, was a very different experience. During the time I lived there, Carbondale had a population of approximately 25,000 people, of which approximately 23% were Black or African American, 6% were Asian, and 3% were Latinx. One of the appealing facts about SIUC was that the school had a large number of African American students, many of whom were from Chicago. As I previously mentioned, I was aware of SIUC's proud and storied history of educating psychologists of color. In spite of being in a small midwestern city, the psychology department did not have trouble attracting students of color. I felt a sense of responsibility to continue that legacy by creating a strong community and sense of family for the students of color in all of the programs in the psychology department.

Even from afar, Dr. White helped to create a family environment by subtly instilling his values to individuals such as myself who were faculty so that we could look out for his people. For example, Dr. White contacted me and told me about an Asian Indian undergraduate student at the UCI, Nima Patel, whom he had been mentoring. He had helped her to select doctoral programs to apply to, and the SIUC counseling psychology program was one of the programs he recommended. Dr. White had given me a heads-up that she was applying, and he spoke very positively about her and how she needed support. After reviewing her application, I agreed, and we extended her an invitation to interview. Later, as Carbondale was a two-hour drive from the nearest major airport, which leads to an expensive van ride or having rent a car, I decided to pick her up at the airport to bring her to Carbondale for the interview.

One of the decisions that I made early in my career was to have a genuine, authentic relationship with my students of color that minimized power distance and the traditional hierarchy between professors and students. Now in case I am misunderstood, let me clarify that this does not mean that I did not create boundaries between myself and students of color. I was not their "friend" in the sense of being a confidante or sharing personal, intimate details about my life. However, I did not treat students of color in a hands-off, depersonalized manner. I wanted my students of color to see me not as simply their professor but also as a down-to-earth human being, someone they could identify with and relate to. One of the ways that I did this was to have social gatherings at my home (which in those days was first an apartment and then a townhouse). These gatherings were potluck dinners where students would bring some type of food or beverage of their choice, and I would provide the main course along with other items. (One of the dishes that I was known for was my meatballs!) It was in the comfort of my home where students of color could metaphorically let their hair down and just be themselves. We would have such a good time eating, drinking, and just being our authentic selves. Students got to see not Dr. Kevin Cokley but simply Kevin Cokley, along with my passions and sometimes vices (I used to drink wine coolers, which, in retrospect, now seems disgusting to consume malt liquor)!

Sometimes there would be a major boxing match, and I would invite students to watch the match. The students would see me stand up, yell at the television, and on occasion "shadow box" as I passionately cheered my favorite boxers. I'll never forget the night when my boxing hero, Roy Jones, was knocked out by his nemesis Antonio Tarver. I was so distraught that I literally ran out of my home! The students witnessed all of this and shared many laughs over my antics. I remember listening to the sounds of neo-soul and dance hall reggae as we enjoyed each other's company. These gatherings also provided students the opportunity to talk about their experiences in the department without fear of judgment or retribution. As students of color, they shared a bond and very much appreciated the opportunities to get together and fellowship with each other. These times felt very much like being with family.

Giving Students the Joe White Treatment at Conferences

One of the signature things that Dr. White did was to create what he called "the Set," which was a nightly informal mentoring session that would be held in the lounge of a hotel, typically a Marriott hotel. There Dr. White would "hold court" among his many mentees. The Set would typically involve providing food and drinks to the invited guests. I remember always being so happy to be a part of the set and envisioning the time where I would be in a position financially to do the same thing for my students. It took several years, but I finally got there financially where I could do this. To be clear, while I'm emphasizing being financially secure enough to treat my students, one does not need to have the finances to be able to create a Set where you engage in an informal mentoring session. However, for me this was something that I very much wanted to do. So when I was financially able, I started telling my former and current students that I wanted us to find a time to get together at conferences over a meal. In some instances, former students may not know current students, so it is a time for them to get introduced to each other. I tell them that I am paying for the meal and drinks, which often takes them by surprise given the number of people involved. Few things bring me more joy as a professor than being able to do this for my students. It helps to deepen our bond and sense of family. In fact, it is the conference experience where my students proudly tell me that when they introduce themselves to people and tell them that they are my students, they are referred to as "Cokley's kids." I have developed a reputation for bringing a lot of students to conferences and supporting them. I am very proud of this reputation. I learned a lot from Dr. White about how to support, nurture, and mentor students in conference spaces.

Conclusion

In this chapter, I have discussed the importance of creating community to support students of color, and I have shared the impact of Dr. White's example on how to support, nurture, and mentor students of color. Writing this chapter has helped me see all the informal ways that Dr. White mentored me, thus expanding my definition and understanding of mentorship. I hope this chapter provides insight into how faculty can create community for their students of color.

Discussion Questions

1   What are examples of how Dr. White created community and provided mentorship for students of color?
2   What creative strategies can you use to create community for students of color?
3   How can you help students of color struggling with impostor feelings?

References

Angelis, T. (2016). *Game changer.* Retrieved on February 7, 2021 from https://www.apa.org/monitor/2016/01/game-changer

Clance, P. D., & Imes, S. (19780. The impostor phenomenon in high achieving women: Dynamics and therapeutic intervention. *Psychotherapy: Theory, Research and Practice, 15,* 241–247.

Cokley, K., Awad, G., Smith, L., Jackson, S., Awosogba, O., Hurst, A., Stone, S., Blondeau, L., & Roberts, D. (2015). The roles of gender stigma consciousness, impostor phenomenon and academic self-concept in the academic outcomes of women and men. *Sex Roles: A Journal of Research, 73*(9–10), 414–426. https://doi-org.ezproxy.lib.utexas.edu/10.1007/s11199-015-0516-7

Cokley, K., McClain, S., Enciso, A., & Martinez, M. (2013). An examination of the impact of minority status stress and impostor feelings on the mental health of diverse ethnic minority college students. *Journal of Multicultural Counseling and Development, 41*(2), 82–95. https://doi-org.ezproxy.lib.utexas.edu/10.1002/j.2161-1912.2013.00029.x

Cokley, K., Smith, L., Bernard, D., Hurst, A., Jackson, S., Stone, S., Awosogba, O., Saucer, C., Bailey, M., & Roberts, D. (2017). Impostor feelings as a moderator and mediator of the relationship between perceived discrimination and mental health among racial/ethnic minority college students. *Journal of Counseling Psychology, 64*(2), 141–154. https://doi-org.ezproxy.lib.utexas.edu/10.1037/cou0000198

Scherer, D. (2020, May 13). *At Texas A&M school spirit is mandatory.* The Culture Crush. https://www.theculturecrush.com/feature/howdy-duty

White, J. L., & Parham, T. A. (1990). *The psychology of Blacks: An Afro-American perspective* (2nd ed.). Englewood Cliffs, NJ: Prentice Hall.

3 Intersectional Allyship & The Importance of Relationships

Jennifer L. Lovell and
Randi E. Scott-McLaughlin

First-Person Narratives

Figure 3.1 Image of Jennifer Lovell and Joseph L. White at the 2011 American Psychological Association Convention in Washington D.C. Provided by and used with permission of Jennifer Lovell (2022).

DOI: 10.4324/9781003132899-4

Jennifer L. Lovell

I excitedly looked at Dr. White. He was sitting across from me at a small bistro table in a hotel restaurant – lights dim – talking about relationships and progress on my Master's thesis. We were attending the Black Male Summit, and I felt deep appreciation because he brought me and a group of other graduate students to the conference. I also felt a sinking feeling in my gut – a confusing mix of anxiety, guilt, righteousness, and imposter syndrome. Why would he waste his valuable time and money on *me*, a white cisgender woman? I was taking up space; shouldn't he mentor someone Black instead? We met when I was a first-year graduate student at Southern Illinois University, Carbondale. I attended one of his invited lectures and was enamored by his vibrant personality and humor. One of his mentees introduced me afterward, and I spoke with him about how I was grappling with my whiteness and whether or not to engage in research with South Asian women (an understudied population in psychology). He listened, affirmed me, guided me toward some additional resources, and invited me to follow up with him based on my decision to move forward. I learned that it was as much about the research process as the outcome. We vibed well together, and he invited me to join him for dinner with a group of mentees. I felt uncomfortable because I did not want to impose on a sacred space for his mentees when these spaces were rare in academia. Dr. White had spent decades engineering a "Freedom Train" of ethnic minority mentees from California to Illinois for PhDs in psychology. Being invited to dinner also felt personal and intimate in a way that challenged my understanding of "professionalism." However, I felt compelled because he trusted me enough to invite me into his sphere, and I decided I would not let my discomfort hold me back. Accepting his invitation solidified our connection. Dr. White was a leader in diversifying the field of psychology, but I was yet another white person in a profession dominated by white women. Tonight, I felt compelled to ask him, "why mentor me?"

He looked over his glasses and gave me an iconic "umh" grunt. His poignant and exaggerated eye blink slowed my racing heart and made me smile. "Well, Jennifer, it's important to have allies. Eh?" I settled in my seat. This was obvious. I realized I was wasting energy feeling guilty and worrying about being worthy when I needed to think about how to genuinely be in *transformative relationships with others* for social justice change. Dr. White was skilled at creating cohorts/coalitions of mentees doing anti-racism and healing work. He told me he was strategic and intentional when bringing together mentees. Although he focused on racial/ethnic identity and gender, he also built his awareness and solidarity with other marginalized groups (e.g., based on sexual orientation, ability). His solidarity felt like a warm embrace. During our conversations, he would ask about my family and my well-being. When I went through a significant loss in my life, Dr. White sent me flowers and a card affirming my strength. His mentorship helped me transform white guilt into a sense of agency to be in allyship with others. He connected me with an academic family. Overall, he demonstrated deep care and a holistic approach to mentorship, and he expected me to do the same for others.

Randi E. Scott-McLaughlin

Note: The following narrative is written reflecting my formative identity process during the time I knew Dr. White. Initially, I identified as a Black man and then as a gender fluid Black person. *After completion of this chapter, I came out as a Black woman.*

In the first year of my counseling psychology PhD program, I was standing in front of my conference poster presentation, and a friend of mine, another Black man, came to me and whispered about Dr. White. I hadn't heard of him before this moment, but my friend told me to come

Figure 3.2 Image of Randi Scott-McLaughlin and Joseph L. White at the 2015 American Psychological Association Convention in Toronto, Ontario. Provided by and used with permission of Randi Scott-McLaughlin (2022).

over to the table where Dr. White was holding court, as I often found he would, with a group of students who were seeking mentorship. By the time I was able to look for Dr. White, he had moved on to somewhere else, but I was searching specifically for a Black male psychologist to help me navigate what I had found to be a challenging first year. It's now the final day of the conference, and I had been unable to see Dr. White, and I did not know what he looked like either, so it was doubly difficult to find him. I was leaving the conference as it was over, and while he was holding court with another group of students, he saw me and called me over with a wave of his hand to sit. He hands me his card, tells me to call Edna, and set up a phone call with him, and he would help me and provide mentorship. I spoke with him at length, he sent me books to read on Black fatherhood as that was an interest of mine at the time, and he encouraged me to attend the next American Psychological Association (APA) convention where he would introduce me to his group of mentees.

Throughout my years in my program, I would continue to schedule calls with him through Edna as I talked with him about how to form my professional identity in psychology as one of the only Black men in my program at the time. I felt isolated, and he encouraged me to form a community of like-minded students. At this time, students were feeling incensed after the Travon Martin and Eric Gardner cases that had recently been in the news, and we were organizing protest events and pushing for more support from our institution. As is true in any group of people, I was quickly faced with how to manage competing interests and how to identify allies. Whenever I asked Dr. White in my phone calls with him how to manage disagreements among my activist student body, he would tell me to look for what you all agree on and focus on that. The central focus and unifying component will rally together people who might disagree on specifics but agree on the overarching goal or mission of the group. Focusing on unification made it easier to identify allies, plan the next steps with my activist peers, and find my voice as a Black psychologist.

Analysis of Narratives

Authoring this chapter on allyship does not mean we (Jennifer and Randi) are excellent allies or experts on allyship. We are writing from our experiential knowledge and reflections on what we learned from Dr. Joseph White and others who have written about – and shown up as – allies in our lives. Based on the teachings of Dr. White, we define *intersectional allyship* as a lifelong and laborious process of (a) building authentic relationships across differences, (b) attending to the uniqueness and wholeness of each person based on their intersecting identities of privilege and marginalization, and (c) using one's privilege and power to support and be in solidarity with marginalized individuals and/or groups of people.

Allyship involves internal transformation (e.g., catching biases, seeking knowledge and self-awareness) in addition to social transformation (e.g., actions and behaviors that disrupt oppression and foster greater compassion). In the following sections, we elaborate on important themes from our allyship narratives and experiences. We then provide practical strategies for being in solidarity with others, and we end the chapter with questions to spark reflection and dialogue.

Authentic Relationships

Dr. White saw caring and personal relationships as a cornerstone for allyship and action, and he was exceptionally skilled at relationship building. He was involved in the civil rights movement and was a champion for educational reform (e.g., Black Studies, Educational Opportunities Program), and he remained engaged in activism throughout his career at the individual, interpersonal, and structural levels. Throughout his activism, Dr. White was skillful in building coalitions and connecting with people. Dr. White would ask personal questions, express care, and *listen intently*. Listening and remembering what people shared was one of his superpowers. On our phone calls, he would share updates and accolades related to the achievements and struggles of other mentees. He knew people's strengths, skills, and areas of expertise, and he attempted to build upon these strengths by linking people together for learning and community building. Importantly, he would also laugh and celebrate with us. His attention to intimate and personal relationships challenged white supremacy, dominant cultural values, and professionalism within academia.

By making relationships personal, Dr. White was able to bring people together. For example, Dr. White encouraged me (Randi) to find points of shared values and unification when identifying allies and people I could work with on issues around campus, such as police brutality, the murder of Eric Garner, and the killing of Travon Martin. Racial justice was a theme I worked on throughout my activities with allies. There would sometimes be disagreement about what exactly should be done or the most effective advocacy strategy. These moments could – and did at times – lead to gridlock that stopped our forward momentum toward the goal of racial justice at the university level, department level, and classroom level. In those moments, Dr. White would encourage me to look for the common thread, the area of agreement. He would ask, "what do you all agree on?" Then he guided me to keep circling back to that key point to provide clarity and focus to our efforts.

Authentic relationships also require building trust. Dr. White had faith in the goodness of people, but he also had a "healthy suspicion of white folks" (White, 2002). *Healthy suspicion* is an adaptive level of distrust based on historical and present-day oppression and discrimination, but trust can be built. Thus, people in Dr. White's inner circle were expected to demonstrate their trustworthiness and dedication to racial justice and positive social change (e.g., via mentoring others, engaging in activism, paying it forward). Observable behaviors help determine who is an ally in any given situation. Accordingly, allyship is not a permanent identity but something that is continually evaluated based on the quality of the relationship and the ways one "shows up." Dr. White modeled how to build authentic relationships in a professional setting, which influences our (Jennifer and Randi's) current work because we place value and importance on building relationships with mentees and colleagues. Authentic and trusting relationships sow the seeds for continual learning and action.

Continual Learning and Intersectionality

Another pillar of allyship for Dr. White involved continual learning. Being in *allyship* or *solidarity with others* (i.e., ally as a verb) is life work rather than a static identity. Dr. White understood the power of working with diverse groups and learning from one another. He was also attuned to the ways power and privilege could impact relationships and group dynamics. In this way, he was attuned to intersectionality (Crenshaw, 1989) in understanding that racism and sexism experienced together is greater than either alone. Positionality matters, and he wanted allies who would work together to amplify Black and Brown voices rather than take over (e.g., white savior mentality). Dr. White put his wellness first and did not make white mentees or allies his priority. However, he viewed allies as integral and integrated into a complex understanding of how to forge bonds between people.

Humility and self-reflection are important when engaging in continual learning. Dr. White acknowledged he would make mistakes and expected that each of us would make mistakes that unintentionally harmed others. Understanding microaggressions and engaging in repair was something we attempted to do as we worked on being allies with one another. From our observations, Dr. White's approach to mistakes was leaning in and engaging in dialogue rather than "calling out." He was not perfect, and he believed no one could be "perfect" in their attempts to be an ally with others. Dr. White talked about seeking knowledge and understanding of other Black folks and ethnic minority groups he worked with (e.g., South Asian, Latinx). He was also working on his own awareness and ability to ally with female mentees navigating sexism and issues important for lesbian, gay, bisexual, and transgender individuals. I (Jennifer) remember Dr. White joking about what I would "tell my mama" about the Black man inviting me to dinner. Although lighthearted, his jokes touched on the reality that he, as a Black man, was putting himself in a vulnerable situation by choosing to mentor me, a white young woman. He saw oppression as multifaceted and intersectional, and he wanted to build a trusting group of people who could work together to make positive change through mentorship and allyship.

Each of us has our own personality and style in enacting allyship, which may shift based on our identity development, professional status, and life transitions. For example, motherhood has profoundly impacted my life (Jennifer), which permeates my role as a mentor and how I engage in allyship with others. I have chosen to continue specific racial justice work at my institution during maternity leave (e.g., facilitating interracial dialogues), but I have also needed to be selective in my engagement and patient with myself as I navigate this life stage. I was mentored by Dr. White when he was Professor Emeritus with adult children, and it is important to note that his approach to mentorship and allyship transitioned over time and evolved. My experience was similar and different compared to his other mentees across time. Allyship is a process of lifelong learning and continual action.

Action with Accountability

To act in allyship or solidarity with others involves identifiable behaviors and actions. Following a conference or workshop, Dr. White would ask his mentees about their experience. Who did they meet? Who would they follow up with? What were the big takeaways from the experience? These questions prompted us to reflect and identify next steps for action. Our sharing was often done in groups so we could learn from each other and also hold each other accountable (note: this was a hallmark of Dr. White's "court" sessions following an event). This is a practice we (Jennifer and Randi) continue with my mentees and undergraduate students. We also try to model the reflective process and share our own reflections on privilege that frame our understanding of the world. Our responsibility is to take action across numerous areas of our life to make changes for social justice.

There are many examples of *performative allyship* in our culture today, whereby a person in privilege talks the social justice talk but does not follow through in meaningful ways. People who do social justice work need to center the needs of those who are being marginalized or oppressed rather than their own needs or desires. Although our liberation is tied to one another, true allies do not engage in social justice work because they want to benefit from it (e.g., advancement, praise, admiration). Allies are working from a place of privilege, and so it can sometimes be easy to step away from the work. Thus, it is important to identify mechanisms for maintaining motivation and holding oneself and others accountable for actions and the impact of our actions.

Ally accountability involves taking responsibility for concrete actions that serve and support a person or group you seek to partner with. Being in allyship is a *skill* that can be developed, and accountability is a mechanism to receive corrective feedback for improvement. Thus, accountability should be a continuous process of checking in with the group you are allied with. This recursive process allows for flexibility and adaptiveness based on the needs of the people you are allied with. Ally accountability is measured by observable behaviors of how one uses their privilege to benefit and partner with a marginalized group. Thus, an important part of allyship is having specific goals and plans for action. Accountability can take the form of informal check-ins with a friend, accountability buddies, and/or a formal accountability plan with designated constituents. Having various forms of accountability is helpful for continued personal growth and effective action.

We emphasize the connection between allyship, action, and accountability because the label "ally" is often misused as an identity label rather than being used to refer to a continual practice (McKinzie, 2014). Mia McKinzie (2014) argued in her essay "No More 'Allies'" that she rejects the term *ally* and instead prefers the use of phrases such as:

- "currently operating in solidarity with ..."
- "showing support for ..."
- "using my privilege to help by ..."
- "demonstrating my commitment to ending [insert oppressive system] by ..." (p. 139–140)

These phrases require examples, and examples are based in action. Thus, if people use the term *ally*, it must be tied to actions for which they are held accountable.

Practical Strategies

Based on the aforementioned themes, it is important to think about allyship from two vantages: (1) the ally and (2) the one being allied with. In the following sections, we share some practical strategies that can help both groups based on what Dr. White taught us through his mentorship and lived example.

Being in Allyship or Solidarity with Others

Caring about a social justice issue can be a motivating force for engaging in activism and allyship. Motivation may also stem from caring (or loving) a person in your life who experiences the negative impact of racism, heterosexism, ableism, ageism, sexism, or other forms of oppression. Motivation can also come from awareness around national or global issues (e.g., from the news). If you feel motivated to make a change and act in ways that show solidarity, then here are a few suggested strategies:

- *Listen generously and share your experiences when invited.* Listen to people's stories, believe people's experiences, be fully present, and work toward deep understanding. Dr. White believed listening was an essential skill for collaboration, understanding, and connecting with others. When invited to share, it can also be helpful for allies to speak about their experiences. Be careful not to dominate or make it all about you, but your experience matters. Sharing can help build authentic relationships and provide credibility and understanding to those who you are allying with.

- *Know your strengths.* Understanding your strengths and competencies will allow you to step up or refer out. You can serve as a conduit and linkage for another person. This will keep you engaged with your advocacy and avoid paralysis due to feeling you are not doing enough. Social justice will not be served by inaction; however, being a link, a connector, and a unifier is valuable.

- *Honestly assess your level of commitment and the amount of risk you are willing to take.* Risks could be social (e.g., ostracism), interpersonal (e.g., tense relationships with others in a group of privilege), financial, emotional, or professional/organizational (e.g., retaliation for standing up against systemic injustice). Being aware of your level of commitment and risk tolerance serves two purposes:

  1) *Identifying your position within a social justice struggle.* By engaging in a higher level of commitment and risk, you may be considered an "accomplice" or "co-conspirator." This could involve street activism or forceful institutional change that breaks down systems of oppression.

  2) *Avoiding over-commitment and burnout.* Being an ally involves a choice. Those who are being allied with are keenly aware of this fact, and they likely have experienced allies supporting them then disappearing when things get hard. Thus, allies need to take on what they can follow through with and not overcommit themselves. Dr. White gave his mentees permission to take space for slowing down, recharging, and engaging in self-care.

- *Prepare for mistakes and/or rejection from those you seek to ally with.* Do not assume you will be embraced simply for showing up once or twice; you need to consistently show up and engage in repair if you make a mistake. If someone shares that you have hurt them, they trust you enough to let you know they expect better. Apologies can be helpful, but actions and changing one's behavior are essential.

- *Identify how your liberation is tied to that of others.* Pulling from Paulo Freire's (2014) *Pedagogy of the Oppressed*, identify how your own humanity has been limited through the dehumanization of the oppressed group you are seeking to ally with. Understand your own story and how you have come to want to be in allyship with certain people or groups of people.

- *Acknowledge your limitations as an ally*. Be humble and be aware of the limits of your knowledge. Being an ally is determined by those you are seeking to ally with, and not something you can self-appoint. Engage in continual learning and stretch yourself. You'll get stronger as an ally the more you practice it.
- *Work with other allies and those in privileged groups*. The world needs more allies to carry the weight, and every little bit held is helpful. It is important to work with others, and specifically with others who are privileged. For example, if you are a white person, it is important to work with other white people to challenge racism. If you are male, then it is important to work with other males to challenge sexism.
- *Avoid harm*. What drives you to do this type of work? If it's for personal accolades, then you are inadvertently engaging in harm. If you're finding yourself feeling overwhelmingly pessimistic about the future fight for liberation, then you might be burning out and potentially edging toward allyship that could be harmful. If you find those you are seeking to ally with seem to become frustrated with you, then this is a cue to check in authentically with those you're allying with. Learning about, and attending to, power dynamics is important when engaging in solidarity with others.

Seeking Allyship from Others

What do you do when looking for an ally yourself? There are intentional ways to look for allies and to understand what you want from an ally. Here are a few considerations when empowering yourself and seeking an ally:

- *Determine what type of ally you need*. Consider what kind of support would be most useful for you. If you are in need of someone who will advocate for you in a predominantly white space and feel like your voice has been silenced or unheard, then you might want to find an ally who can amplify your voice. Communicate with this person about the desired goal and develop a strategy (e.g., have them introduce the topic, or speak about it with you there). When looking for a certain type of advocacy or allyship, try to ask for clear and specific action. This will allow you to evaluate whether or not the person can follow through and show up for you in additional ways in the future.
- *Ask how your ally developed an interest and dedication to the social justice issue*. Dr. White would often share stories about why being a mentor was so important for him and why he created a mentorship network. Similarly, when working with a new ally, it can be helpful to ask them how they came to this point in their life. Why do they care about this issue? What happened in their journey that led them

to connect with you on this particular issue? Not only will this give you a greater sense of understanding of this person and their commitment to the work, but it will also help forge a relationship built on authenticity and personal connection.

- *Share personal stories.* If comfortable, it can be helpful to share personal stories to connect with potential allies. Observe how they respond to your sharing, and use this as a tool for building relationships.
- *Identify points of agreement.* Dr. White recommended identifying shared experiences, values, and goals to help bring people together for change. When conflict in personality or power arose, he encouraged us to find the unifying force to facilitate collaborative planning.
- *Seek a network of allies.* Often, the allies we have are imperfect. You may want an ally who can fight for your equal treatment; however, that is not always who we have available to us. That does not mean lowering your standards of allyship; it just means sometimes you need to collaborate with whomever you can. Or, as my (Randi's) grandfather would say, dock at "any port in a storm." The ally you find may not be all that you wish them to be, but they could link you with others. Thus, it is optimal to create a network of allies within and outside your organization who can support your needs on a more holistic level. Each ally has their own strengths, and as Dr. White would often remind us, it is important to build on people's strengths.
- *Evaluate an ally's ability to take feedback.* As you are working with someone who is seeking to be in allyship with you, pay attention to how they receive and respond to feedback. It may be normal for someone to have a little bit of defensiveness but see how they move through it. Can they receive your feedback or criticism with humility? Do they make a positive change in their behavior? If someone cannot take feedback, then they may not be far enough along in their personal growth to be a dependable and trustworthy ally.
- *Avoid "allies" who do harm.* There is a difference between an ally who cannot meet your needs and an ally who is harming you or movement toward your goals. Also, what one person would consider harm is different from another and will likely depend on your identity development, personal history, and level of social support. With that said, one red flag is if the "ally" is dismissive of your experiences or defensive when you speak about your lived experiences. In seeking allyship, protect yourself from potentially traumatic "allies."

Being an Intersectional Ally

Reality is complicated, and people have multiple identities that are both oppressed and privileged. This can make it such that you are an ally in one instance, while in others, you are the one being allied with. You might even find that you are both receiving and providing allyship in different contexts with the same person. A mutuality occurs in real allyship, and quite literally, you can both be liberated and be the liberator for each other. This type of dynamic can be incredibly powerful when acknowledged and harnessed. Furthermore, as a person from a marginalized group, you might be in a more powerful position (e.g., administration, mentor, policy maker) and able to ally with other members from your own group who need help navigating challenging situations.

When you are enacting allyship, it is important to resist the urge to defend your privileged identities with oppressed ones. It can be alluring to ignore one's privilege and only focus on oppressed identities, almost as a way to defend against feeling or honestly looking at one's limitations. This can lead to dynamics where you oppress others on your journey toward liberation. Thus, it is important to reflect on the privileged identities you hold and how these identities influence your engagement with liberation practices.

Lastly, we are going to end where we began. Dr. White was a storyteller, and he embodied his grandmother's legacy as a "storefront preacher." His rhythm of speech and personal stories pulled people in, and he used his stories to illuminate bigger points of understanding. Storytelling is a tool for understanding oppression and intersectionality, engaging empathy, and connecting with others. Dr. White reminded us that action and change can take time, and sometimes engaging in self-care is an act of disruption. As a graduate student, I (Jennifer) remember Dr. White singing to me on the phone one day, his rendition of an old hymn:

> Keep a-inching a-long, Keep a-inching along. Change will come by-and-by. Keep a-inching a-long, like a poor inch worm, come inching along.

I keep this in mind when I try to force change or become impatient with myself or the world. There is a time and place for urgency, but there is also a time and place for slowly moving forward, one step at a time, keeping the faith that we will get there – together – through authentic relationships, continual learning, and action with accountability.

Discussion Questions

1   Share a story of how an ally has shown up in your life.
    • What was it about this ally that worked well for you? What didn't work well?
2   Share a story of how you've acted in allyship with others.
3   What does solidarity look like, sound like, and/or feel like to you?
4   What was your path to allyship, why was it important for you, and how might you use your story to help others from your privileged group become allies too?

5   How might your identities of privilege and oppression influence the ways in which you act in solidarity with others?
6   How has your own humanity been limited through the dehumanization of the oppressed group you are seeking to ally with?
7   How do you – or how can you – hold yourself accountable for engaging in social justice work?

Land and Space Acknowledgment

Jennifer wrote this chapter while residing on the homeland of the Ohlone Costanoan Esselen peoples (inclusive of Monterey Band, Rumsen, and Carmeleno tribal members). The land and people were brutally colonized starting in the 1700s. Since that time, Monterey has been the home to many ethnic groups (e.g., Spanish, Chinese, European, African American, Japanese, Filipino). Beginning in 1917, the land was used by the U.S. military for training, and it became Fort Ord from 1941 to 1994. Dr. Joseph White completed his basic training at Fort Ord during his two years of military service in the 1950s. The environmental destruction caused by discarded artillery and toxic leakages is part of the Fort's legacy on the land. The Fort was closed in 1994, and part of the land became California State University Monterey Bay (CSUMB). I have a picture of Dr. White in his army uniform in my office, and this reminds me of my personal connection to this land. Furthermore, one legacy of Dr. White's allyship with ethnic minority and first-generation students was his establishment of the Educational Opportunity Program (EOP) within the California State University system.

Randi wrote this chapter while living on the land of the indigenous Lenape tribe that today would be called Harlem, New York. This area was previously referred to as Lenapehoking by the Lenape, and these indigenous people were forced out by the Dutch and British settlers during the 17th century. Contrary to popular belief, New York City was not sold to the Dutch settlers but was thought to be a land-sharing agreement. Since that time, Harlem has been the predominant home of many groups such as the Jewish community, Italian Americans, and currently, Black and Latinx communities.

References

Crenshaw, K. (1989). Demarginalizing the intersection of race and sex: A Black feminist critique of antidiscrimination doctrine, feminist theory and antiracist politics. *University of Chicago Legal Forum, 1989* (1), 139–167. http://chicagounbound.uchicago.edu/uclf/vol1989/iss1/8

Freire, P. (2014). *Pedagogy of the oppressed, 30th anniversary edition*. Bloomsbury.

McKinzie, M. (2014). *Black girl dangerous on race, queerness, class and gender*. BGD Press, Inc.

White, J. L. (2002). Successfully mastering the journey: Psychological challenges facing black male youth. In *Institute on Domestic Violence in the African American Community Conference*. Philadelphia, PA.

Additional Resources

Numerous scholars and change makers have written "dos" and "don'ts" for being a good ally. Here are some of our favorite resources:

Anti-Oppression Network. (n.d.). Allyship. https://theantioppressionnetwork. com/allyship/

McKinzie, M. (2014). *Black girl dangerous on race, queerness, class and gender*. BGD Press, Inc.

Singh, A. A. (2019). *The racial healing handbook: Practical activities to help you challenge privilege, confront systemic racism, & engage in collective healing*. New Harbinger Publications, Inc.

University of Iowa Libraries. (2021). *Anti-racism: Resources for anti-racist allies*. https://guides.lib.uiowa.edu/antiracism/allies

Section II

Paradigm Change – "Making Something from Nothing"

4 Embodied Liberation

Engaging in Activism

Adisa T. Anderson

Figure 4.1 Image of Adisa T. Anderson and Joseph L. White. Provided by and used with permission of Adisa T. Anderson (2022).

DOI: 10.4324/9781003132899-6

Activism Defined

As this chapter will focus on activism, it is necessary to delineate the term "activism" briefly. Activism is simply taking action to effect social change; this can occur in a myriad of ways and in various forms. Often it is concerned with how to change the world through social, political, economic, or environmental change. Activism consists of efforts to promote, impede, or direct social, political, economic, or ecological change or stasis with the desire to make improvements in society and to correct social injustice. Individuals can lead these efforts, but it is often done collectively through social movements.

First-Person Narratives

I will share three different first-person narratives that were paramount interactions with Dr. White and influenced my understanding of activism. Before sharing the narratives, it is essential to share some significant background about Dr. White. Dr. White is known as the "Godfather of Black Psychology." He earned this title through his tremendous contributions to the field of Black Psychology. Dr. White contributed to the success of many students of color and worked as an advocate to reform the education system. He was instrumental in establishing the Education Opportunity Program (EOP), a program that spans all 23 California State University (CSU) campuses.

EOP was created in the late 1960s to overcome economic and social barriers that prevented racial and ethnic minorities and underrepresented students (e.g., low-income, first-generation college students) from attaining a college education. Additionally, Dr. White was one of the founders of the Association of Black Psychologists (ABPSI) in 1968. In 1970, he wrote a seminal article in *Ebony* magazine titled "Towards a Black Psychology." This article helped alter the perception of Black Psychology and elevated it to more mainstream levels in society. The article brought to light the unique differences in how ethnic minorities should be treated and understood in psychology (American Psychological Association, 2012).

Now that you have some brief essential background about Dr. White, we will refocus on the narratives. Although Dr. White and I had had periodic meetings since we first met in 2006, the first significant interaction I will share occurred in Spring 2008 when I received the Joseph L. White Award at the University of California, Irvine (UCI). Soon after this, Dr. White and I scheduled a meeting to discuss transitioning to my doctoral program at Washington State University (WSU) after graduating from UCI. We tried to have quarterly check-ins as I approached graduation, during which Dr. White was always supportive and seemed happy to see me. He was an extension of my family, especially since he mentored

Dr. Thomas Parham. Dr. Parham is another prolific Black psychologist who is currently the university president of CSU Dominguez Hills and previously worked with my father as a staff member at UCI.

For more context, Dr. Parham is also one of the prominent Black psychologists and administrators at UCI that I was blessed to receive valuable mentorship from starting in undergraduate school. Before attending UCI in 2003, my father, Adisa Michael Anderson, worked at UCI from 1980 to 1989. He was a professional staff member in the UCI Admissions Department (Early Outreach) and Junior High School Partnership Program Director. When my father and Dr. Parham met in the 1980s, Dr. Parham was a pre-doctoral intern at the UCI Counseling Center. Dr. Parham and my father were part of the UCI Black Faculty and Staff Association. My father, Dr. Parham, and other Black, indigenous, people of color (BIPOC) faculty, staff, and students were the activists on campus during that time who worked together to address issues of diversity and multiculturalism. They followed the 1960s, where Black students and faculty were in the vanguard of liberation battles over education during the Black Freedom, civil rights, and Black Power movements, advocating for issues such as the inclusion of Black and ethnic studies at predominantly White institutions (PWIs). While terms like "anti-Blackness," "BIPOC," and "LGBTQ+" were not in the vernacular of the university in the 1980s, Black staff like my father and Dr. Parham worked to address some of the same needs back then that Black students face at PWIs today.

During a decade of the 1970s, PWIs were challenged to hire more BIPOC staff and faculty and increase the recruitment enrollment levels of BIPOC students. The California legislature created the TRIO programs within the University of California (UC) and California State University (CSU) system. The TRIO programs served junior high school and high school student populations and operated to expand the college recruitment pool in BIPOC communities. My father specifically worked within the TRIO programs to recruit more BIPOC junior high school students to UCI. Dr. Manuel Gomez was the director of the Early Outreach office, where my father worked. He eventually became the first person of color to serve as the director of UCI's admissions office. He later became the first vice-chancellor of the university student affairs, which Dr. Parham would take on after Dr. Gomez retired. Suffice it to say, the path that contributed to Dr. Parham's rise within the academic community was established by the generations of BIPOC communities that preceded him, like Dr. Gomez, my father, and other more senior Black students, staff, and faculty.

Given this significant history and the intertwining paths of Dr. White, Dr. Parham, and my father at UCI, I always felt honored and privileged to be connected with older Black men who could act as role models in the mental health profession. It was significant that I had several generations of Black men guiding me. I was fortunate to have a robust social support network at UCI and across the country. It felt like divine fate that I would attend UCI, where my father previously worked and where Dr. White and Dr. Parham became my mentors.

During the meeting that Dr. White and I had in spring 2008, he congratulated me on my academic accomplishments. We discussed the importance of pursuing a doctorate in general and attaining a doctorate in Counseling Psychology, especially as a Black man. I shared my doubts and concerns about being accepted by doctoral programs, as I did not have what I thought was the standard package for applicants (i.e., a 4.0 GPA and high standardized test scores), though I had about a 3.6 GPA and decent standardized test scores. Dr. White made several points. One of those points was that although it is prestigious to pursue a doctorate, institutions and degrees do not define one or determine their potential. After our meeting, I reflected on the significance of Dr. White's words, realizing that I was born with inherent value just by existing and did not have to prove my value to any institution.

The second significant interaction with Dr. White that I will share occurred in the fall of 2013. Dr. White and I met via phone to discuss applying to pre-doctoral internships as I was nearing the end of my doctoral studies. I shared with him that while trying to gather tips and strategies for the internship matching process, I spoke with numerous people about the process. Many people (e.g., family, mentors, faculty, colleagues, students) were supportive and encouraging, while other well-intentioned people (e.g., faculty) were discouraging. These well-meaning individuals told me to "think realistically" and "have backup internship options," implying that I was not competitive enough to match my top choices. I knew that the faculty members who expressed these sentiments questioned my competence due to their lack of multicultural awareness and inability to understand and nurture my full potential as a Black man at earlier points in the doctoral program. This experience (e.g., being denigrated as a Black student, viewed as inadequate, invalidated) unfortunately happens far too often to Black doctoral students and other BIPOC students in doctorate programs at PWIs.

For more context, I am originally from Long Beach, California. After living in Pullman, Washington (the northwest), for six years while working on my doctorate, I hoped to return to California by matching for a pre-doctoral internship in the state. However, California tended to have highly sought-after pre-doctoral internship sites. Looking at my pre-doctoral internship list of places to apply, over half of the internships were located in California; I also included some less competitive out-of-state sites. I was advised to use this approach to balance my list and ensure that I successfully matched. In fairness, it was good advice, as the number of doctoral students applying to pre-doctoral internships outnumbered the available positions, and matching is not guaranteed.

Though I was confident that I would match, I was concerned about whether I would match at a top pre-doctoral internship in California. When speaking to Dr. White, I shared that applying to pre-doctoral internships had particular significance for me, as I had encountered some challenges earlier during my doctoral training. I explained that while I had many supporters during the difficult times, I was sometimes discouraged by others who doubted my potential. I felt like the underdog and had something to prove by matching at a top internship. Hearing this, Dr. White explained that others' perceptions do not dictate my potential. He reminded me to "Keep the faith." He helped me to see myself from a strengths-based perspective. Specifically, he noted that although I spent more years working on my doctorate than initially planned, this was a blessing in disguise. Specifically, additional years allowed me to gain significantly more hours of counseling and research experience, develop a clearer sense of my personal and professional identity, clarify my career goals, and network with more counseling center training directors over the years at national conventions.

Dr. White noted that these factors ultimately made me an even more competitive pre-doctoral internship candidate than other applicants with less experience. He also reminded me about the importance of self-determination. Dr. White encouraged me to let my goals and aspirations be self-determined rather than overly influenced by others' limited understanding of my potential. I continued to reflect on Dr. White's meaningful words after the meeting. Through hard work, dedication, and perseverance, I eventually received an impressive ten pre-doctoral internship interviews with primarily top California pre-doctoral internships. Additionally, I matched for a pre-doctoral internship with my top choice at the University of California, Berkeley (UCB) – Counseling and Psychological Services (CAPS).

The third and last meaningful interaction with Dr. White that I will share occurred in October 2016 during our phone call check-in. For context, this was another pivotal time in my career. I completed the pre-doctoral internship, earned a doctorate in Counseling Psychology in 2015, completed the demanding postdoctoral fellowship at UCB – CAPS in July 2016, and applied for career psychologist positions at multiple reputable universities counseling centers. My interviews went well, so I was offered career psychologist positions at various counseling centers, including UCB – CAPS. However, the career psychologist positions were contingent offers that depended on me completing the psychologist licensure process. The licensure process requires applicants to pass national and state exams.

During a phone call with Dr. White, he congratulated me on completing the postdoctoral fellowship and receiving multiple job offers. I shared with him that while I felt proud of these accomplishments, I worked diligently to complete the daunting licensure process but had not passed the national licensure exam on the first try. I explained that I missed passing criteria by just a few points and felt devastated after studying for months. I told Dr. White that I was experiencing the most pressure I had ever had in my career. It seemed as though everything I had worked for depended on completing the licensure process. I did all that I could to maintain a positive and constructive mindset throughout the licensure process. However, the fear of being perceived as a failure felt paralyzing at times, making it more challenging to focus.

Dr. White listened to my concerns, and I could feel his sage wisdom and supportive spirit through the phone. He had a skillful way of instilling hope and always being able to assure me that things would work out. Even when I experienced self-doubt, his deep belief in me helped me persist. Dr. White helped me to reframe my perspective. He reminded me how far I have come, my more significant purpose, and the generations that preceded me and sacrificed so that I could be here. Dr. White noted that standardized exams are often culturally biased. He added that exams are just one assessment of a therapists' competence but not a total reflection of one's potential as a mental health professional. His words helped widen my perspective and see that completing the licensure process would have many other long-term benefits beyond the exam completion.

Dr. White reminded me that my accomplishments and the communities I have positively impacted still matter just as much regardless of the licensure process. He explained that the licensure process is another mechanism in the Western medical system that can unfairly advantage privileged communities (e.g., White, high SES) over more marginalized communities (e.g., BIPOC, lower SES). Dr. White also helped me focus on the more positive outcomes of freedom and autonomy attained with licensure.

Dr. White and my late beloved mother, Sakkara Ingrid Thomas Anderson, had similar types of sage wisdom. Sadly, my dear mother passed away from myeloma cancer in September 2020, but her spirit is still ever-present with me. She was the epitome of a strong Black woman, founder of Queens Historical Society, Inc. (a nonprofit cultural-arts-education organization dedicated to preserving African royal history), and one of my critical influencers on activism based on how she navigated life. Dr. White and my mother reminded me of the social-cultural-political importance of being willing to invest in myself as a Black man. I reflected on this as I persevered through the licensure process and was elated to pass both exams eventually.

Analysis of Narrative

In this section, I will analyze the narratives shared earlier so that the reader can more clearly see my process of understanding Dr. White's words and actions. Let us revisit the first significant interaction I described with Dr. White earlier. We discussed the importance of pursuing a doctorate in general and a doctorate in Counseling Psychology specifically. One of Dr. White's points was that although it is prestigious to pursue a doctorate, institutions and degrees do not define doctoral students, determine their potential, or control their impact on their communities. This point was a critical message. In other words, Dr. White was saying, "You cannot seek validation from the oppressor." Hence, we must constantly derive an internal sense of validation and value rather than depending on external factors and institutions to validate and affirm us. This message is important because when one develops the ability to cultivate internal validation, affirm their presence, and understand their value, one reclaims their power and humanity in the world.

Internal validation is even more important for Black people. Whiteness views Black people from a deficit perspective. Additionally, White supremacist practices dehumanize and disenfranchise Black people and desolate Black cultural traditions. Moreover, Black people were forcibly removed from our land of origin in Africa and exploited through the American slave trade for hundreds of years. Therefore, I believe one of the most effective forms of activism is for Black people to affirm and validate themselves and their humanity. In doing so, Black people reclaim their power from oppressive spaces.

Further examining Dr. White's wisdom, I believe the two keywords in the quote mentioned above are "validation" and "oppressor." Given the antithetical differences in these words, Dr. White understood that it was paradoxical for the oppressor to validate those he seeks to control or enact power over. Conversely, it is disempowering for marginalized communities to rely on an oppressor for validation.

When we rely on others for validation, we relinquish our inherent power to define ourselves. Furthermore, mental health practitioners must realize that racial and ethnic minorities and other marginalized groups (women, LGBTQ+, and the disabled) in our society live under an umbrella of individual, institutional, and cultural forces that often demean them, disadvantage them, and deny them equal access and opportunity (Sue, Sue, Neville and Smith, 2022). Dr. White understood very clearly that experiences of prejudice and discrimination are a social reality for many marginalized groups and negatively affect our psyche and ability to successfully navigate spaces such as academia. Thus, he taught us to never rely on institutions for affirmation that were initially designed to dehumanize Black people based on colonial views and White supremacist notions.

As I progressed through my doctoral training, Dr. White's words became more evident to me. At times when I encountered institutions that held values rooted in anti-Blackness and consequently devalued my presence as a Black man, I understood to not rely on these oppressive spaces for validation. I did not internalize these institutions' pathological views of Black men. However, I understood that institutions often lacked the awareness to foster academic environments that truly supported Black men and other marginalized students.

When confronted by instructors who utilized culturally oppressive grading policies to abuse power and demean students, I understood that I needed to affirm myself and speak truth to power in advocating for equitable academic policies and practices. When I felt like I was walking alone on the educational journey, I understood that I was never truly alone. I was always able to cultivate an internal power of affirmation through the most daunting times by channeling my ancestors' strength, mentors, community, and spirituality. Dr. White would say, "Keep the Faith," as he understood that programs and institutions do not determine our potential.

The African proverb, "It takes a village to raise a child," encapsulates the idea that instead of relying on an oppressor for validation, if one must seek external validation, then one should pull this affirmation from empowering community spaces (i.e., family, friends, mentors, fraternity brothers, colleagues, church family, former supervisors, and community members). Dr. White was a significant proponent of utilizing social support and networks to reinforce success, and he was an advocate for and a master of mentorship. He taught that support networks (e.g., mentors, family, colleagues) could see greatness and potential in one even when one struggled to see it in themselves and could help them cultivate essential characteristics, including scholar-activist identities. Supportive calls, affirming messages, speaking highly of you in the community, speaking truth to you, advocating, protecting, uplifting, and praying for you – over time, I understood that accumulating these seemingly small individual gestures of love and compassion made the difference in helping individuals reach their full potential.

While studying for licensure, I started experiencing emotional distress related to various parts of the process, including culturally biased exam content and expenses associated with the licensure process. Dr. White helped provide insight. Through talking with him, I clarified that some of my emotional distress was caused by experiencing parts of the exam process as another systemic barrier to BIPOC becoming licensed mental health professionals.

Additionally, our discussions helped clarify that I perceived culturally biased exam content as microaggressions and assaults on my cultural identity. Thus, I felt emotionally conflicted learning exam material that I perceived as invalidating or pathologizing BIPOC. Dr. White and Dr. Parham reminded me that as a Black psychologist, I am responsible for learning Western psychological theory and practices that are normed on White people while learning Black and other multicultural psychology concepts.

Dr. White explained that understanding psychology from multiple cultural perspectives would help me provide effective treatment to White and BIPOC clients, thus making me a more well-rounded mental health professional. This wisdom helped me make sense of the utility of learning exam content even when it appeared to be obsolete or irrelevant to treating multicultural communities. Dr. White encouraged me as he clarified the purpose of the process; he helped me connect my efforts with my long-term goals and see everything as preparation for the future.

As I continued to work toward licensure, I realized that in my distress, I had failed to use every resource at my disposal. There was an expensive test preparation course that I initially felt was a luxury that I could not afford. When I mentioned the course to both Dr. White and my beloved mother, they reminded me of the importance of investing in myself. They emphasized the revolutionary nature of Black people intentionally investing in themselves and how my attention to nurturing my own growth was in and of itself a type of activism.

Practical Strategies

The following strategies will be organized into two main sections. The first section (Part A) will focus on developing skills to engage in activism. The second section (Part B) will focus on implementing strategies and tactics for activism. Both sections are curated lists that I believe represent many of the most important concepts to understand about activism, based on my extensive experience and research. However, they are not exhaustive lists given limited space in this chapter. There are other strategies dependent on one's perspective about activism.

Part A: Developing Activist Skills

1 Rising activists should start as early as possible by getting involved with social change, social and political organizations, and social movements (e.g., civil rights, Black Lives Matter, voters' rights, women's rights, youth empowerment, LGBTQ+ rights). Remember, it is never too late to start gaining experience in one's efforts to develop activism.

2 Blooming activists should cultivate leadership skills by observing and reading about influential leaders, seeking mentorship and leadership apprenticeships, and then taking on leadership positions to gain experience and refine their leadership style. One can take on leadership opportunities in social change spaces or whatever organization they have access to as long as one starts gaining experience somewhere. Then the experience can be extrapolated to other organizations and social movements. Relatedly, gain public speaking experience and writing experience to help the activist communicate their

ideas effectively as a leader. Additionally, it is excellent if the activist can gain experience serving as a president, director, co-chair, or vice president of an organization. It is also valuable to get experience at various levels of organizations (e.g., secretary, accountant, historian, coordinator, team captain, general membership) so that the activist understands the experiences of multiple individuals throughout an organization and how the different parts work together toward a shared vision.

3   Budding activists should do community service and volunteer to help build character, shape their values, develop a sense of gratitude, and provide one with perspective.

4   Activists should gain ample experience working with various communities and people, especially communities they plan to impact and work with closely. Gaining experience working with multiple communities will help activists strengthen their interpersonal skills, communication skills, and conflict management skills.

5   Activists should reinforce their courage to challenge systems of oppression and promote social justice. Commit to a practice of making decisions in alignment with their social justice values, even when it is an unpopular decision or there might be consequences.

6   Activists must deepen their knowledge of various areas by watching videos and documentaries and reading literature on social change, leadership, activism, social justice, social-political movements, organizing (e.g., demonstrations, protests), public speaking, strategizing, and other topics. In addition, activists would benefit from bolstering their knowledge in other areas, including critical consciousness; power, privilege, and oppression (e.g., racism, classism, gender, ableism, homophobia, xenophobia); diversity, equity, inclusion, belonging, justice (DEIBJ) practices; social justice principles; politics, psychology, sociology, economics, education, and intersectionality, among other topics. Knowledge in many areas helps activists become more well-rounded, multidimensional, and intersectional in their thinking.

7   Activists should also develop expertise. While it is essential to have a general knowledge repertoire of numerous areas, it is also critical to cultivate a specialization in one or more areas, so people will know the topics with which the activist can provide guidance and consultation.

8   Activists would highly benefit from developing their voice. Developing a voice means gaining clarity about the societal issues that one is motivated to discuss, advocate for, and speak about publicly. As one develops their voice, they gain a deeper awareness of the issues about which they have knowledge and expertise and can therefore offer insightful perspectives to influence discussions in organizations and institutions.

9   Activists must identify societal issues and start applying knowledge, skills, and awareness to address those concerns. Avoid merely absorbing knowledge for the sake of having information and appearing intellectual. It is more impactful as an activist if one shifts from theory to practice and applies their knowledge to address societal dilemmas.

Part B: Implementing Activism Strategies and Tactics

1   Utilize effective organizing and leadership skills to help guide others, galvanize support, and unify individuals around a shared vision. Identify your style(s) of leadership, and try to integrate aspects of collaborative, democratic, servant-based leadership styles. Utilize effective recruitment methods. Utilize effective team building and morale-boosting techniques to help unify your organization or group and to help instill hope and increase motivation for attaining your goal. Additionally, delegate tasks to organization members via a strength-based approach to maximize their skill sets in service of the campaign.

2   Understand the importance of messaging, as detailed and specific messages almost always lead to more participation, support, and funding than vague and unclear messages. Utilize effective messaging and framing strategies, including precise, specific language; applying diagnostic and prognostic frames; using master frames with broad appeal; considering the audience; and securing media coverage.

    a   Diagnostic frames diagnose the problem – they tell people what is wrong. Prognostic frames offer a solution – they tell people what they need to do to help.

    b   Use master frames, as these messaging strategies emphasize broad, widely cherished values such as rights, democracy, and freedom; help increase activist recruitment; and boost social movement success.

    c   In considering the audience, understand that one messaging strategy does not suit all contexts. The organization may need different messaging strategies for recruiting volunteers and activists than when the organization is conducting campaigns. The organization will likely need to switch its messaging throughout a campaign. Recognize that different people in different contexts have other frameworks for understanding and responding to the world. The organization's goal is to help a wide range of people understand the movements better. The organization's messaging also needs to change based on the experience and knowledge of the organization's target.

d   Analyze the organization's or the institution's politics to understand ways to navigate complex politics successfully.

3   Activists should understand their inherent value and their value
to organizations or institutions. Activists should use their value to
leverage change, as the threat of losing valuable members motivates
organizations to change practices and policies.

4   Power is what the activist has and what an opponent thinks the activist or organization has. If the organization is small, hide its numbers
in the dark and create a disturbance that will make everyone believe
the organization has many more people than they do.

5   Keep the pressure on. The most effective protest strategies include
regularly mobilizing, combining protests with other tactics (e.g., rallies, marches, town halls) and focused messaging. The most effective
activists have many actions in their repertoire. The false dichotomy
between "working within the system" and "working outside of the
system" is a myth that lacks substance and thwarts our ability to
enact change. The most effective movements use mainstream tactics,
including voting, lobbying, and drafting legislation. Additionally,
they use nonviolent mobilization tactics, including protests, boycotts, civil disobedience, strikes, sit-ins, and rallies.

a   Determine the type of activism to use based on what best supports the organization's goals. There are various types of activism (e.g., creative, social media/digital, institutional, and
financial). There are also different direct actions (e.g., protests,
demonstrations, boycotts, civil disobedience, strikes, sit-ins,
picketing, letter-writing/petitions). Protests are powerful tools
for generating social change, but they are insufficient alone. Protests are most effective when organizations have political allies
and favorable public opinion, coalitions with other movements
and organizations, and other mainstream tactics such as lobbying and voter mobilization.

b   Concerning pursuing social change in the office, there are four
strategies for organizational activism – advocate, subvert, facilitate, and heal. While there are some activists whose preferential
approach is advocating in public, other activists may prefer a
different approach that's less direct and more covert. These activists are sometimes called subverters, and they operate below
the radar, inconspicuously organizing and escalating tensions to
disrupt the existing condition or state of affairs. They sometimes
do the foundational work for advocates by discreetly amassing
a network of allies and doing research. They also might address
changes themselves, perhaps by framing their agenda in a harm-
less manner, such as offering criticism as an inquiry. Alterna-
tively, they may use existing organizational structures or power

dynamics to promote reform, such as filing a complaint with a human resources department or hiring with social justice principles in mind. A subversive approach is less risky than an advocacy approach since the activist operates covertly to avoid the consequences of openly advocating for change.

6 Ascertain the laws, and know your rights when engaging in activism. Learn the rules, policies, and regulations of organizations or institutions, so the activist understands how to advocate and avoid being reprimanded when possible, is aware of the potential consequences of their actions, and knows how to manage legal concerns.

7 Utilize various fundraising strategies to increase the organization's resources and support the sustainability of the organization's activism. Use tactics that leverage resources. Suppose the organization does not have enough resources or followers to host a large boycott that generates media attention. In that case, the organization may want to direct its energy toward another target or use different tactics. Other tactics that can successfully target companies and institutions include shareholder voting and lobbying policymakers. Other effective tactics include mobilizing voters to change the laws that impact institutions, regulatory bodies, certification associations, and public rating systems. In general, direct communication with companies encourages them to make changes.

8 Activists have long used education to proactively give people the skills and knowledge to overcome bias, unlearn harmful habits, and take on progressive activist work. Research has indicated that this is a vital tactic. Educational programs are among the most influential and impactful tactics for reducing prejudice, preventing oppressive behaviors, and encouraging social justice activism in individuals, organizations, and communities.

9 Remember, social change is a marathon, not a sprint. Thus, activists should understand the importance of mental health and wellness while utilizing self-care practices and coping skills to increase sustainability, maintain motivation and balance, and reduce burnout.

10 Activists should try to maintain their credibility and integrity while managing their reputations. Sometimes organizations or institutions might attempt to slander the activists' reputation with false allegations, engage in character assassination, or scapegoat the activist to undermine the movements' progress. However, the activist should maintain their integrity and remain planted in their values, as the truth will eventually surface, and lies will be exposed. Additionally, avoid allowing "respectability politics" to dictate the approach to activism, as it is essential to engage in activism using a decolonial lens.

11 Use activism to challenge oppression and promote social justice issues (e.g., equity, freedom, fairness) rather than destructive and toxic

issues (e.g., capitalism, violence, White supremacy). The best practices for challenging oppression and promoting social justice include adopting pro-diversity policies and practices and tackling the root cause of oppression. Organizations that take a multicultural perspective on diversity – recognizing and valuing differences between people and actively engaging with inequality and identity issues – have lower levels of prejudice and more member engagement, satisfaction, and learning.

Conclusion

In closing, activism can take many forms (e.g., demonstrating, advocating, organizing, lobbying, persisting in and dismantling oppressive spaces). One does not necessarily need to define themselves as an activist to engage in the practice of activism. In a basic sense, activism is about making a difference with what one cares about and loves while improving the spaces and environments one navigates through. One can engage in activism on many different levels (e.g., micro, macro). Additionally, activism can be how one individually or collectively navigates social change. As we begin to channel the spirit of activism within us, we realize that we can all be change agents in addressing the myriad of societal issues. We recognize that each voice shapes our current and future generations' conditions. I believe our activism should be rooted in social justice principles (e.g., anti-oppression, anti-racism, anti-Blackness) to help guide our activism practice. Lastly, in the paraphrased words of Dr. White, as we "stop seeking validation from oppressive" spaces, we liberate ourselves. With liberation, there is a pathway to speak truth to power by defining our identities, determining our realities, constructing our narratives, changing our conditions, reclaiming our power, and honoring our common thread of humanity.

Discussion Questions

1   How do you see yourself engaging in activism throughout your life and in the future based on the chapter? (Keep in mind that there are many different forms of activism, and one does not need to identify as an activist to practice activism).
2   What areas of your life require work to develop your ability to engage in activism and leadership?
3   Which narratives resonated with your life experiences and why? How does this relate to activism?
4   There are many pearls of wisdom to glean from Dr. White's messages. What lessons did you take from his words?

5   What advice would you want to ask Dr. White if you had an oppor-
    tunity to speak with him, and how would this help you and your
    community?
6   What societal issue(s) will you commit to addressing and implement-
    ing the practical strategies? Why is this important to you?
7   Dr. White was a significant proponent of mentorship. Whom can you
    commit to seeking mentorship from and providing mentorship for in
    your life?

References

Featured psychologist: Joseph White, PhD. (2012). American Psychological As-
    sociation. Retrieved February 7, 2022, from https://www.apa.org/pi/oema/
    resources/ethnicity-health/psychologists/white
Sue, D. W., Sue, D., Neville, H. A., & Smith, L. (2022). *Counseling the culturally
    diverse: Theory and practice* (Jeffryes, J., LaLonde, D., Lipson, E., Weyrauch,
    C., Howarth, J., & Gnanamani, U., Ninth Ed.). John Wiley & Sons.

5 If a Shadow Has Been Cast, It Must Mean There Is Light Nearby

Reflections on Joseph Lewis White

William D. Parham

First-Person Narrative

To place the following narrative in its proper context, know that America is currently facing two pandemics, the coronavirus (COVID-19) and racism. Both are equally alarming but one more recently than the other. The coronavirus is real and ravaging local, state, national, global citizenry without regard for race, social class, gender, sexual orientation, religion, or other hallmarks of personal identity. It hit America allegedly without notice or forewarning in the early months of 2020 with all-consuming vengeance. At no other time in history has the American and worldwide healthcare systems been so challenged to the extreme degrees they experience currently. As of September 2020, for example, the number of confirmed cases of coronavirus exceeded 26 million people with close to 900,000 deaths. Nationally, the number of confirmed cases of COVID-19 was nearing 6.5 million with deaths exceeding 190 million citizens. Lastly, in the state of California, the number of confirmed cases is approaching 750,000 with the number of deaths of Angelinos close to 14,000. In short, as of this writing, COVID-19 has taken its seat at the table of conversation about life's varied challenges and shows no signs, at least not in the immediate future, of giving up the seat.

This insidious virus has disrupted lives of children, adults, and the elderly; pushed people to the limits of their emotional vulnerabilities; and compromised national economies, including elevated number of the unemployed, in ways not seen since the Great Depression. The COVID-19 pandemic has contributed to the heightened anxieties, depression, frustrations, traumas, sadness, uncertainty, and life dissatisfactions that were likely always present but hiding in plain sight. Interpersonal violence, child and elder abuse, and hate crimes, targeted especially at Asian communities, represent additional COVID-19 fallout. And the fallout of COVID-19 has yet to peak.

The World Health Organization (WHO), Center for Disease Control and Prevention (CDC), and public health professionals have promoted several strategies for managing the spread of the virus offering recommendations such as wearing facial masks when out in public and at social

DOI: 10.4324/9781003132899-7

gatherings, sheltering in place (at home), social distancing (maintaining six feet distance between people), hand washing, and frequent use of hand sanitizer. The race to develop a vaccine has awakened the global community into unprecedented actions. As the new year begins, 375,000 deaths and 22.2 million cases have been reported nationally, and the number have yet to peak.

The pandemic of racism has been going on for 400 years with varying degrees of urgency to eradicate it. In short, the pandemic is not new, and there has been no race to find a cure. Known as America's original sin, racism, rooted in false narratives of white supremacy, continues to be a cornerstone of systemic inequities witnessed within multiple contexts including economics, education, employment, housing, and access and utilization of physical and mental healthcare services.

Several weeks into the ever-unfolding coronavirus pandemic, the world witnessed a 9-minutes and 29-seconds lynching-by-knee of George Floyd by a white police officer. This horrific scene, which could not be unseen or unfelt, played out in a larger environmental climate of the disproportionate killing of Black men by white police officers, consequentially resulting in the #BlackLivesMatter movement. As facts of the story surfaced allegations of a pre-existing and troublesome relationship between the white police officer and George Floyd added the personal touch to the killing. The killing of George Floyd was the latest in series of white 'cops' killing Black men (e.g., Trayvon Martin, Tamir Rice, Eric Garner, Ahmaud Arbery, Stephan Clark, Botham Jean, Alton Sterling, Philando Castile, Freddie Gray, Michael Brown, Jacob Blake, Daniel Prude) and women (e.g., Breonna Taylor, Atatiana Jefferson, Aura Rosser, Michelle Cusseaux, Tanisha Anderson). The partial list of fatalities, aforementioned, represents snapshots of long-standing patterns of racial profiling, prejudice, and implicit bias within police forces including police unions.

When viewed through the larger lens of social justice, current times continue to witness the growing presence of hashtag activism and identity reclamation movements by communities no longer willing to succumb and surrender to sanctioned mistreatment, invalidation, and abuse. Rather, these groups felt primed and readied to challenge existing ideologies, share their lived experiences, and demand equal rights and protections under the law.

For example, the incessant sexual harassment and exploitation of women, evident in several high visibility cases (e.g., William "Bill" Cosby, Harvey Weinstein, Jeffrey Epstein, to name a few), resulted in the #MeToo and #TimeUp movements. The push to have men join in the fight for equal rights for women led to the birth of #HeforShe movement. The ever-present disregard, and the extreme distain for the LGBTQ community, gave rise to the #LoveIsLove and #Pride movements. Environmentalists, tired and frustrated mainly by political action groups, added their stake in the game by launching #ClimateChange. Collectively, these oppressed, invalidated, and scorned communities had enough of systemically sanctioned mistreatment and abuse and were no longer willing to just accept what are unfortunately seen as all-too-common practices.

A third environmental context situated in the zeitgeist of current times, and one that adds darkness to existing shadows of uncertainty, invalidation, and macro- and microaggressions, partially framed by the two above-referenced pandemics, is the current national executive leadership. The January 2017 presidential inauguration and subsequent first term in office, relative to traditionally marginalized and ignored ethnic, racial, gender, immigration, and LGBTQ communities, has been defined variously as alienating, contentious, controversial, and divisive. That national presidential leadership continued, importantly, to be propelled unchecked by refusal to behave in accordance with acumen befitting persons holding that position. Also characteristic of that presidency is a profile of unbridled and unparalleled vanity, insatiable desires to soak up admiration from anyone willing to share those sentiments, collusion with powerful and corrupted world leaders, and appointees professing Faustian loyalty with measured and less focused attention on their constituencies on whose behalf they swore to represent and serve. The November 2020 election surfaced palatable angst, anger, frustrations, and fear within and across traditionally marginalized communities adding to the darkness of the shadows that already have been cast. Americans voted in a new president despite the petulant and dangerous behavior of the predecessor. Why is the previously mentioned snapshot of America's current social and political profile important to this narrative? Importantly, where does Joseph Lewis White, Ph.D., fit into the picture?

Analysis of Narrative

Dr. Joseph Lewis White had a front-row seat to perhaps the greatest series of social protests ever recorded on American soil, the Civil Right Movement. Framed within resolute affirmations that enough is enough, two decades of voices from African Americans, and later other traditionally marginalized communities, demanded that America live out its creed, "that all men are created equal, that they are endowed by their Creator with certain unalienable rights, that among these are life, liberty, and the pursuit of happiness". During the years circa 1950–1970, white America unabashedly enacted venomous hate, rage, anger, disgust, and vitriol targeting African Americans, using varied tools for control including but not limited to lynching, cross-burnings, murder, voter suppression literacy tests, and Jim Crow laws forcing segregation in public schools, transportation, and in places such as restrooms, restaurants, and drinking fountains. In a heartfelt, compassionate, and compelling letter written to his young nephew, renowned author, philosopher, poet, and social activist James Baldwin penned the following words, depicting the realities that African Americans were forced to endure during those turbulent years. He writes,

> You were born where you were born and faced the future that you faced because you were Black and for no other reason. The limits of your ambition were, thus, expected to be set forever. You were born into a society which spelled out with brutal clarity, and in as many ways as possible, that you were a worthless human being. You were not expected to aspire to excellence; you were expected to make peace with mediocrity.
>
> (Baldwin, J. 1962, *The Fire Next Time*, pg. 7)

Not surprisingly, these systemically sanctioned assaults on human decency, integrity, and morality, anchored in fraudulent beliefs of white supremacy, erupted into one of the most compelling, determined, gripping, and irrefutable demonstrations of resistance against oppression, segregation, and the blatant disregard for basic human rights. Joe White was a product of these traumatic and tumultuous times. Yet, stillness and calm exist in the eye of a destructive hurricane. In like manner, Joe White, like many African Americans, found strength, hope for better days ahead, and a quiet calm fueling his individual and their collective determination to move forward.

It was his will and knack for moving on, forward, and through the storms of civil unrest, discrimination, prejudices, and systemic inequities that made "Joe", as we saluted him as professionals, the model professional I and we sought to emulate. I marveled at 'Joe's' ability to turn stumbling blocks into stepping stones of success. On occasion he shared stories of his lived experiences growing up overcoming expected and unexpected obstacles along the way. He managed to avert the misfortune that snared disproportionate numbers of known and unknown of his African American generational peers who succumbed to the vicissitudes of urban blight ensconced in economic burdens, community violence, underperforming schools, lack of access to adequate physical and mental health care, substandard housing, record unemployment, and an invoice of other situations and circumstances that made you 'wanna holla'. Joe's budding confidence, sense of agency, savvy navigation of obstacles, and ingenuity for translating lived experiences into life lessons represented just a few of the intrapersonal tools he employed throughout his life. I latched on to every observation that subsequently was indelibly etched into my heart and psyche. It was then that I learned the value in being still wherein I would be positioned best to listen and take in information. In later years, I discovered that when the letters in the word 'listen' are scrambled, they result in the word 'silent'. Thus, the best way to listen to outside people and our inner voice is to find moments every day to be still allowing the insights you already have to surface to consciousness.

Lessons he learned from beating the odds garnered from America's wake-up call of social protests were used to pen his legacy as a professor, consultant, author, practitioner of the healing arts, and dedicated mentor to hundreds of university students. I was one of the fortunate beneficiaries of his genius, gentleness, and humility. Not surprisingly, my professional life continues to be framed in services to others in roles identical to ones Joe executed masterfully.

Joe was never one to be full of himself. He exuded a 'regular dude' kind of swagger that disguised one of the brightest, contemplative, and forward-thinking minds of his generation. His down-to-earth and 'every-day-people' demeanor served as his portal into the lives of people, young, old, rich, poor, male or female, and irrespective of a person's faith-based practice. People from diverse backgrounds and from all walks of life trusted Joe and allowed him to enter their space. This, too, I learned from observing Joe across situations and opportunities.

His 'cool', discerning, and perceptive demeanor also doubled as a welcome embrace of all persons who entered his sphere of influence. Joe opened his door to all persons curious enough to learn what many of us already knew to be true. He was the real deal, unparalleled in style, class, and consciousness! And, in his eyes, our individual and collective visibility was never in doubt.

In short, Dr. Joseph Lewis White was adept at entering social spaces, gifted at making himself quietly present, prided himself at accepting people for who they were and what they represented, and remarkable at finding solutions to academic, career, relational, and intrapersonal puzzles that many of us were just beginning to unpack. Somehow Joe made it feel like the pieces our respective life puzzles would, at the right time, fall into place according to some preordained and divine order. I and we never doubted the forecasts in which Joe invited us to believe. At some basic level, perhaps instinctual or call it a 'vibe', I and we knew that Joe's belief in us, and consequentially our beliefs in ourselves, would manifest in forms greater that we had hoped, dreamed, or desired. If not already obvious, I will add that Joe taught me a lot about the world around me and the spaces I occupied within intrapersonal, interpersonal, academic, career, and personal health and fitness arenas. Joe likely never knew, until many years into my professional life, how much of an affirming impact he made on me. A mantra that best captures my connection to Joe until his passing, when paraphrased, invites consideration that when the student is ready, the master will appear. My readiness and eagerness to learn and to be more intentional with my life choices, coupled with Joe's receptivity to seeing me without judgment, with pride, and without doubt that I was going to make something of myself, fueled my drive to do the best of which I was capable.

Joe was not patronizing, pretentious, or a pretender. His authenticity, genuineness, and liking to 'telling it like is' were expressions I and we could count on with 'take it to the bank' certainty. In truth, I and we never doubted the verity of his perspectives, perceptions, opinions, or insights. Joe's truth about the ebbs and flow of life's challenges, all encased and contextualized within bigger picture socio-political realities, felt both instructive and protective. Joe 'had our backs', and we had his. He knew about distractions and obstacles I and we would likely encounter on life's path, and so he equipped us with lessons on which we continue to reflect and rely. I am recalling at this moment his ongoing challenge to me that came in the form of a 'James Baldwin' question; paraphrased, do you want to aspire to excellence or make peace with mediocrity? His challenges were posed during conversations we had when I served as his teaching assistant (TA), when I was applying to graduate school, when submitting applications to internship sites, when exploring different career positions, and when pursuing my interests as a scholar. At every turn, I sought out Joe for his always-wise counsel and guidance, and he responded to every outreach with clarity, compassion, and by asking me to consider which final choice would best position me with the greatest range of options. He was a master of getting me to think through every decision, ponder related consequences, accept decisions once made, and learn from every experience of which I was able to be a part.

His words resonated with me, and that emotional sustenance is what I tapped into throughout my career. I am recalling my election as one of six representatives of the American Psychological Association (APA) delegation asked to participate in the World Conference against Racism that convened in Durban, South Africa, in 2001. Our goal was to contribute to a global document denouncing racism in all its manifestations. The success of our delegation's visit abroad (APA, 2001, 2004, 2005) also proved to be an invitation to the APA for organizational self-reflection and examination of their internal practices and policies relative to systemic inequities.

I am recalling my decisions to serve back-to-back terms as co-chair of the National Multicultural Conference and Summit (NMCS), 2003 and 2005. And, when deciding how best to discover ways to buoy and support professional peers as they engaged in the work of moving the needle of real change within and across traditionally marginalized communities, I heard the quiet whispers of Joe White affirming my movement forward. From its inception in 1999, with Drs. Lisa Porche-Burke, Rosie Phillips Bingham, Derald Wing Sue, and Melba J. T. Vasquez serving as founders, the NMCS has served as a premier gathering of psychologists of color and diverse communities collectively embracing three realities. The first reality is that systemic inequities and oppression, rooted in fraudulent notions of white supremacy, remain as cancerous social ills. The second reality was the ever-present need for psychologists of color and their allies to reaffirm their consciousness relative to remaining current in their awareness, knowledge, and skills needed to combat systemic oppression.

The third reality came in the form of reminders that responding accurately and appropriately to socially sanctioned systematic oppression demanded attention to honest contemplative self-reflection. Apropos to this observation is the oft-heard mantra that a person will never see their reflection in running water. It is only when the water is still will their reflected image begin to emerge.

During my terms of service as co-chair, Joe was one of the first to always acknowledge my efforts to pay it forward. His outreach to me during my time at the helm of these two professional gatherings was as unfailing as his acknowledgments of the impact he felt I was making. His praise for what he believed was a job well done is best captured in at least three proudly expressed proclamations, "Looking good!", "Keep on keeping on!", and "Keep the faith!"

As I look back, I also recall my year as president (2006–2007) of the Society of Counseling Psychology, Division 17 of the APA. Joe was just as supportive, kind, and not surprised by either my election to the presidential office or the projects I introduced for Division 17 for their collective consideration. One of the worst storms to hit American shores came in the forms of Hurricanes Katrina and Rita (2005) that crashed into the city of New Orleans, Louisiana, and the neighboring gulf coast. The haunting devastation, the incalculable emotional turmoil, and the call for community engagement and support were never more visible. One of three presidential projects I initiated was to get Division 17 involved in giving back to residents and communities in New Orleans whose lives were forever changed by the destructive hurricanes. The annual convention of the APA was to convene in New Orleans the year I was president, and I could not attend the convention without using my position to effect change in some small way in the lives of New Orleans residents.

I selected a committee of Division 17 colleagues to champion this project, consulted with them regularly as they contacted a variety of service agencies in New Orleans to learn about their needs, worked with them to concretize logistics (e.g., presentation day and time, and location where activities were to take place), actively participated in two presentations at two different sites, and solicited from program attendees feedback and level of satisfaction with the interventions that were rendered. The collaborative success of the "Give Back" project in New Orleans led to decisions by subsequent Division 17 leadership to replicate, henceforth, the same giveback efforts in every city that hosted the APA convention. Joe seemed especially proud of the longer-term impact I was able to trigger.

I was no less involved with another professional psychological organization, the American Board of Professional Psychology (ABPP), where I served terms as both president of the Counseling Board and then as a member of the Board of Trustees. Of the work in which I was engaged, Joe was aware of an article I authored in 2001, 'The Meeting Is Adjourned: Dismantling the Old Boy's Club within the American Board of

Professional Psychology' (Parham, 2001) wherein I called on the ABPP to self-examine their complicit actions to avoid addressing issues of equity and fairness within and across the organization. Due to his passing, he was not able to read and comment on the latest article I authored, 'There Is No Secret to Uncover or Puzzle to Solve: It Is Time to Play Hard or Go Home' (Parham, 2020), articulating ABPP's failure to make progress since publication of the first article 20 years earlier.

Joe was called home by our Creator on November 21, 2017, following a life well lived. He never learned about other roles I now occupy and in which I serve others. In May 2018, I was asked to serve as the inaugural director of the Mental Health and Wellness Program for the National Basketball Players Association (Fisher, 2020). This role was unique in American professional sports communities. Further, the unprecedented portfolio of services aimed at addressing the mental health and wellness challenges of professional basketball players, and the support of distinguished journalists partnering with us to advance our message, represented the first domino to fall setting in motion clear invitations to other professional sport organizations to begin addressing the mental health and well-being of the athletes who bring their organizations fame and recognition.

Joe's passing also meant that he never learned about my appointment as a member of the Mental Health and Wellness Task Force of the United States Olympic and Paralympic Committee (USOPC). The collective voice of several elite Olympic and Paralympic athletes, across teams, calling for mental health and wellness services triggered an organizational response, the sustainability of which remains to be seen. Joe did know that I was a consulting psychologist for the United States Olympic Committee (USOC) during 1996 Olympics, a role that had me working with the woman's Olympic volleyball team between 1994 and 1996. I suspect that he would not have been surprised by my current affiliation and contributions to the USOPC.

As I continue to reflect, I doubt that Joe would have been surprised by my participation as a member of the International Society of Sport Psychology Think Tank, a group of colleagues across the globe addressing the mental health and wellness of elite athletes (Henrikson, Schinke, Moesch, McCann, Parham, Larsen, & Terry, 2019). Though Joe and I never talked about my latest roles, he is, nonetheless, present in my spirit whenever and wherever I serve.

Continued reflection on Joe's impact on my life is best told in a fable I read long ago that, nonetheless, resonates in my spirit to the present day. As the story goes, two frogs having fun were leaping together in and out of waterholes. Caught up in their excitement and not paying attention, both ended up leaping into a hole that was so deep they could not leap out. Their persistent efforts to leap out of the deep hole in which they found themselves failed and gave way to them yelling and croaking fervidly hoping that other frogs would hear their cries and come to their aid.

Many frogs came, positioned themselves around the deep hole, and began initially to cheer them on. Realizing that the hole was just too deep, the frogs encircling the deep hole yelled to the two trapped frogs to just give up, let it go, and make peace with the perception that the task was just too insurmountable. Both the trapped frogs jumped a while longer until one just gave up and died. The second frog, rested for a bit, gathered his strength, felt stronger, and then commenced to jumping harder and with more focused intent to accomplish his goal. His persistence paid off as he finally leaped so high that he was able to get out of the hole.

The frogs encircled atop the deep hole were amazed at such a stellar accomplishment and, at the same time, puzzled about how the second frog was able to succeed. They recalled telling the second frog to "just quit, give up, and resign yourself to your destiny to forever be in a deep hole". The second frog, now extricated from his former circumstance, thanked the group of encircled frogs for their support and for cheering him on. Once again, the encircled frogs were puzzled as they knew that they were not cheering him on. Their leg gestures and chants were inviting him to give up. Just then, the encircled group of frogs realized that the second frog, now free, was deaf, so it never heard a word they said. You see, sometimes you have to turn a deaf ear to what others tell you is impossible.

I was one of Joe's deaf frogs, not hearing the naysayers, disbelievers, and 'haters and doubters'. Joe seemed to have drawn strength and direction from the very people who never gave him a chance, second thought, or further consideration. In fact, on another occasion, Joe invited me to consider that 'haters and doubters', and, at the extreme, persons who exuded vitriol and villainy, were sharing gifts to be opened. Puzzled, I respectfully questioned his use of the word 'gift' to which he replied, "… yes, that is what I want you to see!" He went on to say that as long as I knew where I was headed with my education, career pursuits, and dreams for success, however measured, the clear and unmistakable stance of persons in my way provided me with the gift of choice; to go around them to the right, to the left, over, or under. In short, the visual acuity of a person's life's aspirations is strengthened when an opposing person truly communicates where they stand relationally to you and on issues of concerns. I have never forgotten that lesson and since that time have opened many gifts. And I continue to do so buoyed by the echoing words of one of Joe's favorite poets, Robert Frost, who, at the end of his oft-recited poem, 'Stopping by Woods on a Snowy Evening' (Frost, 1923), proclaims, "I have miles to go before I sleep, miles to go before I sleep".

Practical Strategies

Returning to where I began this narrative, to say that the current zeitgeist framing 2020 is alarming, shocking, and frightening represents a huge understatement. Arguably, the intersecting and combustible realities of dual pandemics, economic upheaval, and persons young, old, and in between, of all races and ethnicities, reaching the limits of their emotional bandwidths, have created jet streams of clouds formed by confusion, chaos, and controversies that have cast shadows of darkness and doubt. In a moment of stillness, I am reminded of an irrefutable observation which invites consideration that when shadows are cast, it must mean that light is nearby. Shadows cannot be cast without light!

Joseph Lewis White was the light that illuminated possibilities and options. His light also brought hope to spaces wherever life's shadows and darkness had been cast. He reminded me often of one of life's biggest promises that foreseeable as well as off-the-radar challenges, hurdles, obstacles, and roadblocks would inevitably cross my path. True to his always affirming and encouraging spirit, Joe never failed to complete his reminder of life's realities with a companion reminder for me to understand and appreciate my innate abilities, talents, and adeptness to respond to whatever impediments and obstructions would manifest along the life's path. In essence, though we cannot change the direction of the wind, we can adjust the sail.

To young aspirants reading this narrative, always strive to be the best of which you are capable. Do not be afraid to get involved, and situating yourself in service to others is always a good place to start. Offered for your consideration is a mantra that suggests that the best way to find yourself is to lose yourself in the service in others. Securing positions, from support staff to leadership, in professional associations and local, regional, and national conferences or volunteering your services to work in community hospitals, group homes, or elder care facilities represents organizations with which to become engaged.

To colleagues feeling good about their career and life balance, the invitation herein is to ask if current comforts are serving as emotional safety zones of convenience and, thus, precluding discovery of more ways to stretch to new heights and meaningful, other-directed accomplishments.

In practical terms, I am offering several suggestions for consideration. First, find time for genuine self-reflections on a regular basis. Deciding to be intentionally mindful about personal and professional activities in which you engage helps you remain grounded and focused. Second, identify north-star goals, accomplishments you would like to experience ten years from now, for each area in your professional portfolio. Focusing on what you want to accomplish in the near and distant futures helps fuel clarity of vision and determination to see your dreams come to fruition. Third, dream again, as you did as a child, and also allow yourself to match the degree of curiosity you experienced as a youth. In his book *Russell Rules*, Hall of Famer and 11-time NBA champion with the Boston Celtics Bill Russell suggests that curiosity is the oxygen of all success and accomplishments.

Fourth, ask yourself the following question on a daily basis: What one thing can I do today that is better than I did yesterday, knowing that it won't be as good as what I will accomplish tomorrow? Positioning yourself for daily successes leads to weekly, monthly, and yearly accomplishments about which you will be proud. Fifth, push yourself beyond your personal zones of comfort and convenience, which might occasionally involve taking measured personal and professional risks. Success is not always linear, and opportunities to grow and mature, personally and professionally, often surface on roads less traveled. The last suggestion is to be open to surrendering to evaluating personal and professional activities that define the person and professional you are or want to become. The biggest life lessons often come from mistakes and from real or perceived failures. Situations or circumstances are never as important as a person's response to challenge with which they are confronted.

Concluding Remarks

Joe was the gift that kept on giving. My thanks to him for his guidance in helping me discover my place and purpose, and for every ounce of belief he had in me that I would accomplish whatever I set my mind to, has been to pay it forward. Thus, every student I teach and/or mentor, clients to whom I respond when asking for help as they journey to heal, and colleagues with whom I interact represent my investment in them that was akin to Joe's investment in me. Joe was never directly in the lives of the people I now serve. Or could I be wrong? Perhaps, they have met Joe through me and are now receiving glimpses of a remarkable man whose signature kindness, generosity, and humility are penned on the hearts and minds of all other persons who entered his circle on influence. Hmm, yet another reflection on which to ponder.

Discussion Questions

My time with Joe and acknowledgment of the silent and vocal ways he provided encouragement, support, guidance, mentoring, unconditional acceptance, and unbridled belief in my abilities, talents, and genius prompt the following four questions for audience consideration:

1   When listening to a speaker at a retirement event celebrating your long and storied career, on what concrete and tangible accomplishments do you hope the speaker will be able to articulate and elaborate?
2   If you take a moment to engage in honest self-reflection, how much time, on a daily basis, do you set aside to just be still, absolutely quiet, allowing yourself to acknowledge your talents, tap into your confidence, and act intentionally relative to accomplishing established goals?

3 In which professional associations do you hold membership, and how active are you relative to participating in divisional, section, or interest group governance?

4 When thinking about your body of work, how well rounded is your career portfolio? Does it include activities such as teaching, clinical service, consultation, scholarship, or community service? More important, if you had $1,000.00 and had to divide the total amount into the number of activities in your portfolio, how much value, based on the amount of money you invest, do you give to each activity?

These few questions of the many that could be asked invite consideration of a final reminder prompted in no small way by the passing of Joseph Lewis White, Ph.D. Our respective life journeys are finite, and within this limited and unpromised time, we have abundant opportunities to discover innate talents and abilities as well as our life's purpose. Related, if granted 100 years of life on earth, failure to exhaust the endless reservoir of divine gifts and talents with which we have been blessed will be the guaranteed outcome. In short, now is the time to seize every moment of every day with excitement and a renewed sense of purpose and drive knowing that the Creator did not bring us this far, just to bring us this far! So, let me end where I began by asking, if not now, then when?

References

American Psychological Association. (2001). *APA Resolution on Racism and Racial Discrimination: A Policy Statement in Support of the Goals of the 2001 World Conference against Racism, Racial Discrimination, Xenophobia, and Related Intolerance*. Washington, DC: American Psychological Association. (Retrieved from http://www.apa.org/pi/racismresolution.html)

American Psychological Association Task Force on the World Conference against Racism Report. (2005, February 4). *Task force on the world conference against racism report: Findings and recommendations (submitted to APA Council of Representatives)*. Washington, DC: American Psychological Association.

American Psychological Association World Conference against Racism Delegation. (2004, March 15). *Final report: The United Nations World Conference against Racism, Racial Discrimination, Xenophobia and Related Intolerance (WCAR)*. Washington, DC: American Psychological Association.

Baldwin, J. (1992). *The Fire Next Time*. Vintage reissue edition, New York, NY: Vintage.

Fisher, M. (2020). Exclusive: NBPA's Dr. Parham on the NBA and Coronavirus- 'Still Waters' and 'Hidden Tattoos'. Sports Illustrated: Dallas Sports. https://www.si.com/nba/mavericks/news/exclusive-nbpa-dr-parham-on-the-nba-and-coronavirus-still-waters-and-hidden-tattoos

Frost, R. (1923). *Stopping by Woods on a Snowy Evening. The Poetry of Robert Frost*. New York: NY: Henry Holt & Co.

Henrikson, K., Schinke, R. J., Moesch, K., McCann, S., Parham, W. D., Larsen, C. K., & Terry, P. (2019). Consensus statement on improving the mental health of high-performance athletes. *International Journal of Sport and Exercise Psychology*, 1–8.

Parham, W. D. (2001). The meeting is adjourned: Dismantling the old boys club within the American Board of Professional Psychology. *The Diplomate*, 20, 2 (ABPP: Chapel Hill, NC).

Parham, W. D. (2020). There is no secret to uncover or puzzle to solve: It is time to play hard or go home. *The Diplomate*, 47, 28–31 (ABPP: Chapel Hill, NC).

Russel, B. (2002). *Russell Rules: 11 Lessons on Leadership from the Twentieth Century's Greatest Winner*. New York: New American Library.

6   A Radical Shift

Shaping the Next Generation of Scholar-Activists of Color

Jeanett Castellanos, Hector Y. Adames,
Nayeli Y. Chavez-Dueñas, and Veronica Franco

> *Go forth to create new directions to fulfill these unfulfilled hopes,*
> *unfulfilled opportunities, and unfulfilled promises.*
> —Dr. Joseph L. White

Black, Indigenous, and People of Color (BIPOC) in the United States are living through one of the most painful periods in modern history. Between 2020 and 2021, the novel coronavirus (COVID-19) ravaged our communities. It has exposed and compounded what so many of us already knew—that systemic racism is harmful to our health; it is the culprit of our unfilled dreams. More than ever, we need a radical shift. For many of us, education is a catalyst for social change—a way to resist oppression, create a different existence, and realize our hopes. To borrow from Nelson Mandela, "education is the most powerful weapon you can use to change the world" (n.d., para 1). All these are reasons why we need to change and expand educational systems to center the needs and lived experiences of BIPOC students and help develop transformative mentoring relationships.

In this chapter, we reflect on our life-changing relationships with our beloved mentor and ancestor, Dr. Joseph L. White, who devoted his life to radically shifting the educational landscape of the United States. He created spaces for BIPOC students where none existed. For instance, in 1967, he founded the Educational Opportunity Program (EOP) in California, which allowed millions of low-income minoritized students to enter and graduate from public and private colleges and universities. Given the success of his model, it was then replicated throughout the United States. Dr. White also imparted his wisdom to many generations of scholars, practitioners, and administrators throughout the decades through his innovative network affectionately known as the *Freedom Train*. In the following section, we briefly share some of our memories with Dr. White as a prelude to discussing three themes that connect our stories, including: (a) the value of mattering, (b) embracing lessons from our ancestors, and (c) developing and nurturing a scholar-activist identity as BIPOC. The chapter culminates with actionable items to consider and questions to help you reflect and engage in your journey by creating new directions to fulfill your unfulfilled hopes, opportunities, and promises.

DOI: 10.4324/9781003132899-8

Figure 6.1 Image of Joseph L. White, Hector Y. Adames, and Nayeli Y. Chavez-Dueñas. Provided by and used with permission of Hector Adames (2022).

Narratives: The Transformative Power of Connections

The need for human closeness is the deepest of all human needs.
                                        —Dr. Joseph L. White

Dr. White believed in the transformative power of human connection, and through his relationship with us, he changed our trajectories forever. Although the four of us worked with Dr. White at different stages of our careers, we were all shaped by how he fully showed up in our lives. We recall him being authentically himself, beaming smiles, a burst of contagious laughter, and always filled with an abundance of brilliant and high-spirited stories. In every encounter, Dr. White made us feel like we were the most significant persons in the world. He listened and paid attention to our human needs; he validated our sadness, normalized our anger, and celebrated our joy. Dr. White invited us to imagine the impossible for ourselves, our families, and our communities. He believed in our dreams and moved earth and sky to help bring our dreams to fruition.

Dr. White was a giver and what we call the Griot[1] of Mentoring—he loved and believed in the transformative power of storytelling. He shared so much of himself with all his mentees. We recall surrounding Dr. White at conferences and dinners where he passionately told stories from his childhood, his youth days in San Francisco, and his years in academia. Each narrative was filled with lessons centered on the interlocking complexities of race, oppression, and power. Collectively, these stories and moments of connection were a master class. Each story motivated us to critically view the world and think deeply about the poisonous impact of racism and inequities in our lives and the lives of the people we serve. At times, we would go down a path of despair when discussing the painful and inhumane ways BIPOC continue to be treated in academic settings and beyond. Dr. White would listen attentively and constantly remind us that we have "to be able to bounce back from a setback … bounce back and become stronger in the broken places." However, being resilient is insufficient; instead, he also invited us to expand by sharing that "you need not just to recover; you've got to move beyond recovery." The following brief examples from one of his mentees illustrate how he helped us focus on our strengths instead of our fears. The mentee describes:

> I remember being in his office and sharing that I was nervous about taking the GRE (Graduate Record Examinations). He sat there in his chair with his arms crossed and said, "of course, you are worried about the GRE; it is a test that was not created for you, and that triggers a sense of othering." Dr. White proceeded by affirmatively saying, "instead of worrying about a test that says nothing about you—think about your full application." He asked several vital questions such as: How can I get strong letters of recommendations? How can I improve and draft a quality personal statement? Towards the end of our meeting, he gave me the 2016 APA graduate programs book and sent me off on my way. Today, I am a doctoral candidate!

Dr. White wanted us all to thrive. His lessons permitted us to question everything and critically think of innovative ways to better the conditions of our community. These teachings propelled us to devote our careers to creating theories, models, interventions, and mentoring relationships that resist using deficit models when studying and describing BIPOC. Dr. White would explain that "we have the skills that can move us away from the gloom and doom of illness, and the gloom and doom of abnormal psychology, and onto wellness and optimal living." Overall, his mentoring relationship empowered us to own our voice, our strengths, and our power.

Analysis: Taking Charge of Our Destiny

The last challenge remaining for us is to take charge of our destiny as People of Color.

—Dr. Joseph L. White

In reflecting on the many lessons we learned from Dr. White, three themes stand out. In the following sections, we list and describe them. Specifically, we discuss: (a) the transformative power of mattering, (b) embracing lessons from the ancestors, and (c) developing and nurturing a scholar-activist identity.

The Transformative Power of Mattering

The theme of *mattering* centers on exploring who we are, valuing what makes us unique, and knowing what we deserve. Dr. White encouraged us to explore how history, context, and family impacted who we became and the opportunities to which we have had access. He also emphasized the importance of knowing our strengths and how our individual experiences have influenced us. He believed that his job was to "help us love and accept who we are while instilling in us a sense of hope and purpose." Dr. White described that part of being a good mentor was using our talents, skills, and connections to address and remove the internal and external barriers that BIPOC often encounter. Furthermore, he believed that the responsibility of mentors is to help develop networks of connections to enable and open access routes for mentees. His motto was grounded in the principle that people already had what they needed to be successful and that all he was there to do was show up for people, provide support, and be a witness to their growth. He provided us with guidance, reassurance, and a pathway to success or *a game plan* to attain our dreams and hopes. In his eyes, we were all *diamonds in the rough*, simply needing a little polishing.

Mattering also involves understanding that despite our collective histories of oppression; we are valuable. Every single one of us deserves treatment grounded in dignity and respect. He would often remind us that the ways institutions treat us do not define who we are and what we deserve. For instance, Dr. White's most important teachings were "do not seek validation from the oppressor." Through this message, he reminded us that while systems are not designed to reflect and validate our experiences or provide the resources we needed, we could lean on our community and the teachings of our ancestors to take charge of our destinies.

Dr. White also helped us understand that our heritage *matters*. He taught us the importance of recognizing the strengths and beauty of the social groups and communities to which we belong, and he invited us to voice, understand, and internalize our families' dreams. As such, Dr. White intentionally created spaces that nurtured and validated our families, our communities, and the sum of our experiences and identities. He consistently engaged us in conversations about our mothers, fathers, siblings, grandparents, and our communities. He knew our mothers by their names and gave their voices a platform. Dr. White helped us to learn that the experience of mattering is a collective journey that is healing and transformative—we only advance as far as the person in the back of the line moves forward—we are all in this together.

Learning from the Ancestors

Dr. White understood the power of our collective histories filled with the lessons from our ancestors—people who learned how to navigate oppression, survive their subjugation, and despite it all, they dared to thrive. Embedded in our histories and the wisdom of our ancestors is the importance of spirituality, human connections, and strategies for resistance. Connecting or reconnecting with these teachings can help us raise our spirits, fuel our motivation, and inspire us "to keep on keeping on."

The following conversation with our Dr. White reflects the importance of learning from our ancestors:

> Dr. White talked about growing up hearing about the underground railroad and how Harriet Tubman and many others had utilized a network of secret routes, houses, and people to help enslaved people reach their freedom. He was fascinated by how individuals working together could create access routes for other people to free each other. Later in life, he realized that while our bodies had been freed,

Figure 6.2 Image of Joseph L. White, Jeanett Castellanos, Veronica Franco, and other mentees (Mary Dueñas, and Erick Felix). Provided by and used with permission of Veronica Franco (2022).

we (BIPOC) continued to be mentally enslaved in three ways: (a) We lacked an understanding of our history and the strengths of our people, (b) We were not taught the skills necessary to access the networks, and (c) We did not have role models and networks to open access routes for us that could facilitate mental freedom.

Building from the ancestors' wisdom, Dr. White envisioned *the Freedom Train* as a way for people to support each other. He noticed that many of us BIPOC did not dream big, because we had no role models who could show us the way. Dr. White shared how as a teen, all he aspired to be was a waiter to serve white people because he did not know there were other options available to him. His educational *Freedom Train* was his desire to let Youth of Color and young professionals imagine and dream about possibilities. Through the *Freedom Train*, he sought to give people the opportunity to dream about the destination they wanted to reach using the lessons of strength and perseverance that come from our ancestors. For Dr. White, the *Freedom Train* is about building a group of scholar-activists.

Developing and Nurturing a Scholar-Activist Identity

Dr. White demonstrated a masterful ability to help shape a dream and transform a vision into reality. He was devoted to mentoring and nurturing revolutionary scholar-activists who would create new models, theories, and practices that conceptualized BIPOC from a strength-based perspective. Collectively, we recall a story by our mentor who used to say:

> Teach these children how to be resourceful, imaginative, creative, problem solvers ... sometimes, it may take two or three tries to get it together, but it can be done! My mother looked at me, and she said, Make something out of nothing!

Dr. White made something out of all of us. He taught us to recognize the impact of racism on our lives, communities, and respective fields of study. As part of shaping scholar-activists, our mentor consistently referenced the power of community and network. As the quintessential scholar-activist role model, Dr. White helped pave the way by co-founding the Association of Black Psychologists (ABPsi) in 1968 in response to the civil rights movement of the 1960s, which sought liberation and equitable treatment under the law (White, 1984). ABPsi adopted a position of social and political advocacy (see White, 1984). As a founding member, Dr. White challenged the biases inherent in the psychology and aimed to address the specific role that racism plays in the profession.

Today, many of Dr. White's mentees are living his scholar-activist legacy. For instance, one of the authors (Castellanos) was a founding member of the National Latinx Psychological Association (NLPA) and the California Latinx Psychological Association (CLPA). She also instituted the Latinx Student Psychological Association at the University of California, Irvine, and is currently working on a mentorship program to promote the partnership between ethnic professional organizations and psychology graduate programs at the national level. Dr. Castellanos also has a research team of undergraduate scholars who study the role of race in education and psychology. These students learn about strength-based research, write with their mentor, and many pursue graduate school.

Two additional mentees, Chavez-Dueñas and Adames, are the founders and co-directors of the Immigration, Critical Race, And Cultural Equity (IC-RACE) Lab, whose mission is to:

> develop models, programs, and interventions that are designed to promote and support psychological wellness within different Communities of Color... the lab is committed to speaking out against the social injustices that impact Communities of Color, including policies and laws grounded on ethnic and racial hate, disparities in health and education, and the lack of access to resources necessary for individuals' well-being, dignity, and joy... the lab also emphasizes mentorship and promotes graduate student development by increasing knowledge, awareness, and skills necessary for members to become racially conscious and culturally responsive mental health providers, researchers, scholars, and educators.
>
> (IC-RACE Lab, n.d., para 1; see www.icrace.org)

Overall, Dr. White's vision was to facilitate a legacy of Freedom Train Riders breaking through the status quo by using our skills and training to change how BIPOC are studied and treated in the social sciences. Understanding the power of creative scholarship, the importance of shifting the field to be inclusive, and the value of theories and models that include our communities, the authors answer the call to be innovative in our work to promote psychological wellness in our communities. Examples of creative works by scholar-activists mentored by Dr. White include the framework of (a) *The Psychology of Radical Healing* (see French, Lewis, Mosley, Adames, Chavez-Dueñas, Chen, & Neville, 2019) and (b) *Radical Hope in Revolting Times* (Mosley, Neville, Chavez-Dueñas, Adames, Lewis, & French, 2020), which aim to move the field of psychology and higher education beyond deficit-based perspectives. Our work as scholar-activists is to challenge racism in scholarship and build professional spaces and theories that promote a psychology that is for the people, by the people, and accessible to the people. As Dr. White's mentees, we commit to engaging in scholarship that humanizes BIPOC communities and encourages hope in a future free of oppression.

Practical Strategies for a Radical Shift

The following section provides directives for effective practices in shaping the next generation of BIPOC scholar-activists. We offer guidance in three areas described earlier in the chapter: (a) mattering, (b) honoring the ancestors, and (c) developing an activist-scholar identity.

Mattering

> *Mentors need to provide students with relationships where they can feel validated and build confidence. They need to affirm their existence and let them know that they bring something of value to the university.*
> —Dr. Joseph L. White

1   Assist mentees in learning and understanding their group's history in the context of race in the United States. Help them reflect on their social identities and identify the privileges they enjoy compared to other BIPOC members. Address issues of race and culture with your mentee while acknowledging your role in resisting racism in society.

2   Treat your students with dignity and respect while identifying their cultural strengths. Remember that differences do not mean deficiency.

3   Recognize that students' cultural lessons from their homes and communities hold value and offer great blueprints for navigating and succeeding in the academic setting. Encourage mentees to cultivate and maintain connections to their cultural roots.

4   Generate discussions that promote students' understanding of their journeys, the lessons that have contributed to their resistance to oppression, and their ability to balance emotions, mediate adversity, and problem solve. Create validating spaces for the students, their families, and communities that celebrate cultural history, values, beliefs, and practices.

5   Help mentees amplify their voice and show them the value and knowledge they hold. Remind them that their experiences and insights matter. Empower younger generations to use their voice and recognize its importance by hearing their stories, giving a platform to their narratives, and valuing their experiences.
   • Encourage students to engage in scholarship by writing, supporting innovative research, and promoting strength-based practices.
   • Create a research team where students experience community, share experiences and resources, and support one another in their scholar development.

6   Model for your mentees how to effectively share their stories as a way to resist racism, strengthen their resilience, and contribute to the greater good. Emphasize the impact of individual and collective

efforts and the power of creating networks and opportunities that counter inequity and social injustice.

Honoring the Ancestors

Through a shared experience, individuals know they are not alone, that they are psychologically connected to others who can affirm the actuality of their experiences.

— Dr. Joseph L. White

1   The dream is not acquiring material goods; it is collective survival, freedom, justice, and equity. It is the liberation of the spirit and mind. Teach BIPOC the value of intergenerational knowledge, the role of the struggle, and their social responsibility to contribute to the liberation of our people.
2   Help BIPOC connect meaning to their degrees in relation to the collective dream. We are here because others fought for us to be exactly where we are. Centralize race culture and community in the students' work. Connect the degree to the BIPOC students' community and needs. Help their history motivate their journey.
3   Facilitate mental liberation. Direct students to read narratives by Leaders of Color—those who understood the importance of social justice in an oppressive society. Encourage students to address the unjust structures in society. Support community action research and scholarship that elevates the human spirit and address deficit-based models.
4   Validate the importance of interdependent relationships, the role of interconnectedness, and the importance of creating change by learning the lessons of those who came before us.

Developing Activist-Scholars

We need them to become the successful scholars of the next generation. We must take charge to define ourselves, define our own psychology, and build our own psychology that is strength-based and represents the voice of the people.

—Dr. Joseph L. White

1   Unpack systemic racism and help mentees find ways to navigate its impact on their minds and spirits. Help students understand the impact of oppression while recognizing the strength, resourcefulness, and resilience in themselves and their community.
2   Recognize the biases in our current theories and models. Encourage your students to engage in scholarship that promotes and advocates for social change. Model critical thinking, create space for

BIPOC students to challenge the narrative, and identify gaps in the literature.

3   Promote the development of creative and innovative scientific models and theories. Tie the liberation psychology to research and direct your mentees in generating culturally responsive and racially conscious practices and interventions for the field.

4   Support the development of professionals who understand the importance of strength-based research and scholarship, the value of offering counter-narratives, and embrace the essence of being an activist-scholar. Support leaders who promote social change, social justice, and racial justice.

5   Engage in conversations regarding how oppressive the system is and identify ways to navigate a marginalizing culture set in traditional and racist practices. Teach your mentees how to apply theory to practice to problem solve, create programs in their communities, and promote social change.

6   Cultivate community to provide a space of validation, liberation, healing, and radical hope. Cultivate students' sense of being and belonging by disrupting narratives of otherness. Help create networks where BIPOC students feel empowered, use their voice, and dream beyond their communities' stereotypes.

7   Center students' wholeness in the mentoring relationship emphasizing the value of joining networks and seeking collaborative spaces. Help mentees build networks with other BIPOC scholars and professionals who can serve as mentors, help them develop their confidence, learn from their achievements and struggles, and create opportunities.

Discussion Questions

Advancing social justice requires a radical shift, and as Dr. White taught us, the change can begin with us and the relationships we foster with our students. Mentors must recognize the power of personal connection, the role of validation and empowerment, and the centrality of race, culture, and community. Community building, networks, and opportunities must be available to BIPOC students to maximize their potential. Further, training programs must equip activist-scholars with a set of skills to bridge science and practice. This final section provides a list of discussion questions to help educators gain insight into inclusive mentoring practices that center on human connections while acknowledging the significance of race and culture. Guided by the thematic lessons, the following questions help mentors collectively integrate the content (narrative, analysis, and best practices). This reflective activity associates the various lessons to mentors' circumstances and current practices.

Mattering

1   How are you guiding BIPOC students in the process of owning and celebrating their power, knowledge, and uniqueness?
2   What institutional opportunities are you creating to help BIPOC students recognize the power of their narratives?
3   How do you create a community in academia to hold people accountable in creating an infrastructure that facilitates the development of BIPOC scholars?
4   What role are you playing in helping develop networks of connection and empowerment that open access routes for BIPOC students?
5   What literature are you reading to help you understand the racialized experiences of BIPOC communities and the role of power in your students' experiences? How does your engagement strengthen, uplift, and empower the social groups and communities to which BIPOC students belong to?

Ancestral Roots

1   What is the legacy of your ancestors? How are your roots informing your legacy? How is your ancestral knowledge and wisdom guiding your mentoring relationships and scholar identity?
2   In what ways are you inviting and honoring your students' generational knowledge?
3   How do you help fuel the dream and, in return, role model for BIPOC students the importance of dreaming big and dreaming beyond the limitations placed on them by systemic oppression?
4   How does your scholarship, engagement, and community work support and contribute to developing opportunities for your BIPOC students?
5   What opportunities do you create for your mentees to meet other BIPOC scholars and build community? Do these opportunities reflect family-like systems that promote the sharing of resources and promote the professional growth of your mentees?

Activist-Scholar Identity

1   How can you facilitate the development of an activist-scholar identity in your students?
2   How do you help mentees engage in an emancipatory approach that promotes healing for not only themselves but also their community?
3   How do you facilitate scholars' development of a healthy racial identity?

4   What efforts have you put forth to decolonize the roots of your field? How have you worked to include BIPOC voices in the history of the field's scholarship?
5   There is a need for a radical shift in higher education. What will be your role in the radical change? How will you structurally shape the next generations of BIPOC scholar-activists?

Note

1 A griot is a West African storyteller often seen as a leader and advisor who conveys the collective wisdom of a cultural group (see Henrich, 2001).

References

French, B. H., Lewis, J. A., Mosley, D. V., Adames, H. Y., Chavez-Dueñas, N. Y., Chen, G. A., & Neville, H. A. (2019). Toward a psychological framework of radical healing in Communities of Color. *The Counseling Psychologist, 48*(1), 14–46. https://doi.org/10.1177/0011000019843506

Henrich, D. J. (2001). The griot storyteller and modern media. *Communicatio: South African Journal of Communication Theory and Research, 27*(1), 24–27. https://doi.org/10.1080/02500160108537921

IC-RACE Lab. (n.d.). *About Us: Immigration Critical Race and Cultural Equity Lab.* Retrieved from www.icrace.org.

Mandela, N. (n.d.). Nelson Mandela Quotes. *Goodreads.* Retrieved from https://www.goodreads.com/quotes/16243-education-is-the-most-powerful-weapon-which-you-can-use

Mosley, D. V., Neville, H. A., Chavez- Dueñas, N. Y., Adames, H. Y., Lewis, J. A., & French, B. H. (2020). Radical hope in revolting times: Proposing a culturally relevant psychological framework. *Social and Personality Compass, 14*(1), e12512. https://doi.org/10.1111/spc3.12512

White, J. L. (1984). *The Psychology of Blacks: An Afro-American Perspective.* Prentice-Hall.

Section III

Institutional Change – "Getting Strong in the Broken Places"

7 Healing in the Broken Places

Practical Strategies for Leaders and Change Makers[1]

Thomas A. Parham and Gerald Parham

Figure 7.1 Image of Thomas Parham and Joseph L. White. Provided by and used with permission of Thomas Parham (2022).

Opening

Amid the cultural wars between traditional psychology and African-centered psychology (Parham et al., 2011) that have played out in psychological journals, books, academic classrooms, and conference presentations over the past five decades, Black psychologists have been able in

---

1 This article is a chapter in an edited book by Palmer on *Practical Social Justice: Diversity, Equity, and Inclusion Strategies Based on the Insights of Dr. Joseph L. White.* No part of this manuscript may be cited or reproduced without the expressed written permission of the first author.

DOI: 10.4324/9781003132899-10

the past and continue to advance in the present the narratives of a more culturally congruent perspective (Jones, 1972, 1980; Guthrie, 1976; Nobles, 1986; Akbar, 1992). Indeed, the cultural battles they have fought, as Parham et al. (2011) so eloquently describe, were contentions and conflicts involving a war of conceptual ideologies, a war of axiology and values, a war of cultural relevance, and a war over self-determination. They have done so by first critiquing the application of theories and constructs brokered by traditional psychology and its Eurocentric roots to people of African descent. Understand here that the endeavor to provide critical analysis of traditional theories was not an objection to White psychologists being able to speak on their own reality and the life experiences of the broader White community. Rather, the challenge with traditional psychology's practices were their attempts to take theories and constructs developed by and for Euro-American people and apply them to other people of color, especially those of African descent. When that occurred, Joe White and others were clear that many weakness-dominated and inferiority-oriented conclusions emerged and only looked at African American people through the lens of pathology and cultural deficiency (White, 1984; White & Parham, 1990). Those efforts by African-centered psychologists and other multicultural scholars (Sue, 1981; Sue & Sue, 1990, 2003; Ivey, D'Andrea, Bradford-Ivey, & Simek-Morgan, 2002) were followed by an entire body of literature that summoned its most intellectually deep and culturally rich concepts and constructs to frame the worldview from a more African and African American reality. Out of those initiatives, the contemporary discipline of Black Psychology was born.

Dr. Joseph L. White was one of the chief architects of that movement, and the ideas he framed and defended as pillars of the new discipline and field of study have, in fact, served as the conceptual anchors for teaching students; exploring, researching, and confirming hypotheses; and applying culturally grounded principles in the treatment of people struggling with mild, moderate, and severe mental and emotional debilitations. His classic article titled Towards a Black Psychology (White, 1970, 1972) was the seminal treatise that framed the discourse for many scholars who contributed to that extensive body of work. Dr. White was a proud clinical psychologist by training, but to his students he taught and mentored, the patients he treated, and colleagues he advised, helped grow professionally, and befriended, he was a healer. In theorizing and articulating his worldview to the disciplines of psychology, psychiatry, social work, and education, he offered a set of psychological themes that he believed best summarized the life experiences of Black people as reflected in their use of language, oral traditions, and expressive patterns. The six themes he outlined in his early work (White, 1984; White & Parham, 1990) included:

- Emotional vitality
- Realness (keeping it real and telling it like it is)

- Resilience (the ability to recover from and grow from adversity)
- Interrelatedness
- The value of direct experience
- Distrust and deception (of other people's worldview or explanations that invalidated your humanity)

These themes, for him, symbolized the intellectual, emotional, behavioral, and as he would say "cultural flavor" of the Black psychological perspective.

It was out of his articulation of these themes, particularly "realness & tell'in it like it is" and "resilience & revitalization," along with Dr. White's understanding of the human psyche, that the notion of healing in the broken places emerged (White, 1984; White & Parham, 1990). He was clear through his own lived experiences, clinical observations with clients and patients, and listening to the language of the people as expressed in books, poetry, rhythm and blues music, and teaching and learning from his own students in university classrooms that psychological growth was aligned with a person navigating their way through the storms of lived experiences and emerging on the other side of those adversities with a greater awareness of their own vulnerabilities and capacity to overcome the "troubled seas of life." Indeed, the duality of our individual

Figure 7.2 Image of mentees with Thomas Parham and Joseph L. White in the center. Provided by and used with permission of Thomas Parham (2022).

and collective perspicacity allows for the synthesis of opposite where the emotional pain, struggle, grief, and heartache that result from situations and circumstances are balanced by the experiences of joy, laughter, sensuality, and an enhanced empathy for the struggles and triumphs of others. Healing in those broken places, illustrated by our process of recovery and ascendency to new levels of psychological growth, development, and maturity, was a bedrock of those axioms advanced by Dr. White as he instructed and mentored us in the ways of living and knowing.

This chapter is our effort to illustrate how Dr. White's principle of *healing in the broken places* was operationalized in our own lives, as we share interactions and conversations with Dr. White over the course of a 42-plus-year relationship with our teacher and respected elder (Mzee). Coverage is also given to defining this notion of healing from our perspective, chronicling what we believe are some of those broken places in life, and providing perspectives and strategies for leaders and change makers as they seek to operationalize this principle in their own efforts and endeavors.

Personal Interactions

In the seasons of one's personal and academic journey, there are milestone events that mark significant and consequential moments in our lives. For the Parham family, one of those moments began when we met Dr. Joseph L. White. William met him first when he transferred to the University of California, Irvine (UCI), from West Los Angeles Community College to complete his undergraduate studies as a Junior. Gerald entered UCI as a new freshman and met him in 1973; Thomas followed as a transfer student from California State University, Long Beach, in 1975. Joe wasn't just familiar with the Parham brothers (William, Thomas, and Gerald) as students and mentees at UCI but was an integral part of our extended family who knew our mother Sadie Parham, our sister Pamela, her daughter Tiosha Nicole, and other close family and friends. He was invited to share our dinner table at immediate and extended family events, which he sometimes attended, knowing the importance that family played in our lives as well as his own. Thus, Gerald and I have decided to collectively contribute to this chapter and offer our personal insights.

Thomas

For Thomas, his reflections began with Dr. White as a professor at UCI, even before Thomas transferred to UCI during his Junior year. He would sometimes venture down to visit his brothers on campus during 1972–1974 and, on occasion, had an opportunity to sit in on Dr. White's class on the psychology of the Afro-Americans, which was held in the evening hours that quarter. Once officially transferring to UCI to complete his undergraduate studies, he actually enrolled in Professor White's course. He remembers that

> as a classroom professor, Dr. White became larger than life. He was intellectually gifted yet spoke to me and other students in a soulful vernacular and language that was authentic, genuine, affirming, and that we could all understand. Beyond having one of the finest conceptual minds of anyone I have ever met, he had the ability to break down complex concepts in a clear, understandable, and sequential fashion. Joe could take a vast number of disparate constructs and somehow synthesize them into coherent themes that helped all in attendance at his classroom or conference lectures consolidate the information. Not surprisingly, I became a willing, obedient student to his teaching, and managed to perform well in his class on African American Psychology.

A month or more after completing that African American psychology course, a chance encounter with Dr. White on the ring mall walkway on the campus of UCI changed the trajectory of my life, T. Parham reports.

> In approaching Dr. White one early afternoon as we were coming from opposite directions, I addressed him as respectfully as any student would and said, "good afternoon Dr. White." In responding to my greeting, he simply moved closer to me, put his arm around my shoulder, and said "young brother, you have too much talent and you are too brilliant to be running around here playing basketball and chasing women. Come follow me." As I walked with him a hundred yards or so toward the Social Science building where his office was located, he invited me to make an appointment with Edna Mejia, his secretary, to meet with him.

That meeting, which occurred about a week later, was a life changing event for Thomas. He reports that during that meeting,

> he sat me down, raised questions about my background, interests, and aspirations, as well as my academic performance to date outside of his class I had recently completed with an "A" grade. After listening intently, he then turned his attention to 30" × 20" chalkboard adjacent to his office desk and began to diagram my whole future on that board. From directives to "tighten up my grades" to produce a more consistent standard of excellence across all classes I was taking, to invitations to serve as his undergraduate teaching assistant, to plans to pursue a Masters and Doctorate degree in my post-graduate education, the blueprint for my professional life began to unfold.

In the meetings that followed, Dr. White used those occasions to assess progress on specific goals given to Thomas, build on those directives with additional invitations, and take the occasion to dispense pieces of wisdom and knowledge that were born out of Joe's own experiences with life. These stories and anecdotes included accounts of growing up and family life, parental socialization, primary and secondary educational pursuits, attending college, personal and intimate relationships, activism in the civil rights and Black power era, his own educational ascendency to become a doctoral-level psychologist, exposure to discrimination and oppression, child rearing, factors and social practices that served as stumbling blocks along life's journey, his belief in the inherent worth and talent students of color possessed, how to manage one's finances in adulthood, definitions of responsible manhood, and his formula for managing one's mental health.

These occasions of sharing and reflection were more than teachable moments; they served as implicit and explicit opportunities for socializing young men in much the same way a father would talk with his son. When more experienced adults decide to share their knowledge and worldliness with younger generations, it is a special space born out of the ways men come to know what they know through living. It parallels directly with a principle Joe always talked about in classroom lectures and in his writings related to the "value of direct experience" (White & Parham, 1990). The reference to a father–son relationship here was not far from the bond Drs. White and Parham developed. Indeed, the two developed bonds of closeness, trust, admiration, and support that carried them through over 42 years of living, collaborating, creating, and engaging life with all of its joys and pains.

The bond that Joe and Thomas were able to form emerged out of more than a mere student-professor relationship. To hear Dr. White tell it (White & Parham, 2015), his invitation to Thomas to be his mentee was formed out of a recognition of shared experiences growing up in America. Both were Black males, raised by single parents where their father was absent, each family unit was economically challenged, both were raised in urban centers in America, both had interest in and were involved in athletics, each was intellectually capable, and each of them had a mindset on helping others. These bonds of connectedness were the soil out of which their relationship grew. The Jegna-student relationship that evolved over the years became the basis for numerous interactions in the classroom, advising and counseling other students, attending and presenting at conferences, Thomas serving as an undergraduate teaching assistant in Dr. White's course, clinical supervision while Thomas was a doctoral psychology intern, and a whole range of life decisions that would further enhance the friendship both Drs. Parham and White enjoyed as mature adults.

Gerald

For Gerald, he had a great relationship with Dr. White as well, and in similar ways, it was anchored in bonds of closeness, a recognition of latent potential, and a belief that he as a new university student, and later a maturing adult, could manifest his goals and dreams at what Joe referred to as "the next level." Gerald reports that he first heard of Dr. Joseph L. White in 1973, his senior year in high school when on occasional weekends, he would come down to UCI from our home in Los Angeles to visit our oldest brother, Dr. William Parham, who was a student. Our brother being a psychology major (Social Ecology) was also a mentee of Dr. White. However, it was not until Gerald came down to UCI the following year (fall 1973), to begin his undergraduate tenure at UCI, that he met Dr. White. Gerald remarks that

> my first impression was a bit of a surprise as I had a very different image of him than the man I met. His small stature and distinctive voice were things I had not expected, yet I could not help but listen to him as he shared strategies for success to a small group of incoming minority students. We were participants in a summer bridge program designed to orient us to the collegiate experience. Dr. White spoke of the composition of the campus community, which in 1973 was very different than the diverse urban environment where I had grown up in the City of Los Angeles. His words provided me with a sense of comfort; a feeling that along with my brother, I was going to be ok.

It was also during that time that Gerald and Joe had occasion to talk and ponder thoughts about who he was and what activities he was interested in engaging on the Irvine campus. He inspired Gerald to apply for and become a resident advisor and subsequently run for office in the Associated Students of UCI (ASUCI) as the vice president, Administrative Services. This position provided Gerald with access to the senior executives of the university in ways other students did not enjoy and provided him a great introduction to the world of networking. That introduction on how to effectively engage and collaborate with influential adults was an important lesson in what Gerald describes as the "who you know" part of life's political dynamics.

Gerald further remembers that after his undergraduate career, he worked in the private sector for a few years until 1980. During that mid-1970s time frame, he was contacted by Dr. White who arranged for him to secure a position with the Department of Commerce, Bureau of the Census. Gerald recalls that

> I was the Field Operations Supervisor, overseeing all census operations between Seal Beach and San Diego County. In this capacity, I had oversight of 700 plus staff. It was after this experience that he

rolled me in the political arena, working as a volunteer for President Jimmy Carter's election campaign in 1976. He showed me how to get the 700 folks I had worked with to continue to work with me in this endeavor. I ended up going from volunteer to paid status and was subsequently invited to the inauguration in January of 1977. He knew what he was doing. After this project he talked with me about my next steps and encouraged me to go to Law school, believing at that time that we had enough psychologists in the family. I wasn't really keen on that idea, so I pursued graduate work in Counselor Education at the University of Florida.

Upon his return to California in 1998, which Gerald considers a blessing, Dr. White was one of the first individuals he connected with. Over the next ten-plus years, he and Joe spent several lunch hours discussing what his administrative role on campus should be given his position in residence life and how to use his skills in building relationships to develop programs that were beneficial to the student population he was serving. Gerald also remarked that

> Joe was always supportive of my efforts, even to the point of agreeing to deliver a keynote address at a student housing conference of which I was a program chair. I will never forget his many sayings in that unique Dr. White voice, that exclaimed, "You're looking good dude" followed by "Keep the faith". I will forever be grateful for his mentorship and guidance, for his belief in me, his friendship, and overall relationship with my family.

Personal Reflections and Experiences

Becoming a Teaching Assistant as an Advanced Undergraduate Student

When Thomas was invited to serve as a teaching assistant, along with his brother William, they would often meet over a meal before the evening class began. Those mealtime occasions were an opportunity to discuss the curriculum for the week, any special points of emphasis that needed to be reinforced, upcoming deadlines regarding tests and assignments students needed to be reminded about, study and review sessions we needed to proctor and lead, class projects and tests that needed to be reviewed and graded, and any challenges with the course that enrolled students may have been experiencing. Once we all arrived at the course, in ways similar to a professor with his or her entourage in tow, the announcements would be given, the lecture would begin, questions would be answered, and the students were as engaged with Professor White as any could be.

Beyond managing the course logistics however, the ritual of "break-ing bread" also allowed for a level of sharing and discussion that pro-vided further opportunities for the sharing of Joe's wisdom. It was during those occasions that the concept involving the need to "heal in the bro-ken places" was reinforced. In talking about male-female relationships, the ebb and flow of joy and pain was a place where people needed to heal. When talking about the constructive and sometimes dysfunctional ways people chose to deal with their adversities in life through substance, we talked about the need to heal. When student performance was being negatively impacted by a diminished sense of self and efficacy, we talked about the need for healing. On one occasion, where Thomas was invited by Joe to work with a woman with a terminal illness to manage her af-fairs and living situation as she prepared for her eventual passing, there was a need to help her psychologically heal and reconcile her blessings to date with the cruelty life had brought by rendering her a terminal disease and diagnosis. During the mid-to-late 1970s, when oppression, racism, discrimination, apartheid, and police abuse and injustice were rampant, there was a need to help both the victims of that oppression and society itself to heal. Unquestionably, the invitation to serve as a teaching assis-tant for two years was a very meaningful and impactful experience for Thomas.

Walking the Streets of New York

During the annual rituals of professional conference attendance, Dr. White and Thomas (while Thomas was a graduate student from a Midwest university) had occasion to stroll the streets of New York City, outside of their participation in the conference's programming that year. That circumstance provided yet another occasion for Dr. White to impart his wisdom and share his own challenges with navigating the circum-stances in life that helped him grow as a husband, father, psychologist, and Black man in America. In those anecdotes were the particular stories of his developmental years growing up in a single parent inner-city fam-ily, childhood loves, experiences in undergraduate and graduate school, his experiences as a husband and father to three children and maturing young ladies, his experiencing housing discrimination as an early career professional, his involvement in social movements (i.e. Black power and civil rights) and political campaigns (Sen. Robert Kennedy's run for pres-ident), crystallizing his own identity as a psychologist and person of Af-rican descent, and the pitfalls one needed to avoid along life's journey in seeking opportunity and success. That occasion was also a bonding moment for Joe and Thomas. That moment and their own sharing and reciprocal exchange allowed both men, one the lifelong student and one the professor, to cross a boundary of respectful social distance to a place where trust, genuine caring, and empathy served as the bridge to deeper levels of understanding and authenticity. Several specific recollections Thomas recalls from that occasion included a conversation regarding the development of conscious manhood and helping to distinguish between being a male by virtue of one's gender and a socially conscious Black man as a result of one's experiences and decisions at critical choice points.

Another set of teachable moments from that evening's stroll through the city revolved around the observation that too many careers of prominent African American people had been derailed by their involvement in less than constructive behaviors. These included the overuse of alcohol and substance, involvement in simultaneous relationships with women, financial challenges that resulted from not being a good steward of one's financial resources, and believing that one's success entitled individual Black men to the same privileges, courtesies, and opportunities as his White counterparts. In Dr. White's reflections and observations were admonition to Thomas to ensure that he avoided those pitfalls, as each could lead to a broken place ushered in by personal decision making and behaviors as opposed to any societal or external element that instigated the trouble one could find themselves in.

The Loss of Our Dear Mother

Perhaps no single event in our lives was more emotionally impactful and painful than the loss of our dear mother, Sadie Parham. She made her transition to the realm of the Ancestors in July 1998, ten days shy of her 76th birthday. Beyond being a single parent raising four children by herself, our mother was a self-sacrificing woman who lived for her children. Her principal focus was the care and safety of her children while denying herself comforts and convenience to ensure that our basic needs for nutrition, shelter, clothing, schooling, and spiritual upbringing were met. Even in our transitions from children to adolescents, adolescents to young women and men, and developing into more mature adults, she always kept a watchful eye on our personal, professional, and even financial health.

Not surprisingly, as the elder years and medical ailments began to take their toll on her own health, we prepared for a time when GOD would call her home and reward her with a place in eternity she had sacrificed for and prayed about with daily frequency. And yet, not surprisingly, even though the intellectual rehearsals and emotional anticipation of what that moment and space in time might feel like, no amount of anticipatory affect could prepare us for the emotional pain losing her would bring. And as the days, weeks, months, and now over 20 years have passed, we continue to remind ourselves about the need to heal in the broken places, and the life lessons and teachable moments echoed from our memories of Dr. Joseph White.

A Recent Loss of a Lifelong Friend and Dr. White's Mentee

During the months and final days of writing this chapter, we have experienced another loss that leaves our spirits hurting and very low. The broken heart we are feeling at the loss of our dear friend and brother Dr. Aldrich Patterson is deep and profound. It is yet another example of how we will need to heal in the broken places of life, with a hope to emerge on the other side of our grief and emotional pain with some measure of comfort. Dr. Aldrich M. "Pat" Patterson was a high school friend of the Parham family. Given the alphabetical order of his last name, he sat behind Thomas throughout four years of high school in the late 1960s and early 1970s. Pat was like another son to our mother and has been a part of our family for some 52-plus years. Like us, he completed his undergraduate studies at UCI and went on to pursue his doctorate in counseling psychology at the University of Maryland, College Park. Upon completing his degree, Pat was hired as a staff psychologist in the psychological counseling and wellness center at California State University, Chico, where he served from 1983 until his retirement in 2014, after 30-plus years of service. In his retirement, he continued to see and treat patients in his private practice in Chico, California.

His passing, captured in the pain and tears we all feel and shed, forces us to dig deep into the reservoir of our faith, compassion, memories, and love. In those spaces, as we come to terms with the loss of a friend, colleague, and decent human being, healing will come from reflections on the joys we experienced as youth, young adults, and mature professionals. There is the recognition that we never took our friendship and brotherly love for granted; that even in conversations and text messages in the final year, months, and days he walked this earth, we were able to share how much we loved each other as brothers; how we hoped for better days in managing our respective health conditions; and how we looked forward, along with other friends, to opportunities to fellowship face-to-face, once the current COVID health crisis subsided and allowed for more personal engagement. Mostly, we are reconciled that we do not have to couple the pain of his loss with the tragedy of regret, knowing that there was nothing we wanted to say or do for each other in this lifetime that went unsaid or undone. That is a message for leaders and change makers who are able to guide people to engage in verbal and behavioral interactions that lead to initiating the process of healing while also preparing individuals and groups for the inevitabilities of life's painful and tragic moments, and the proactive postures one can assume that minimize the suffering and distress once those events do impact people's lives. In these moments, some three years since Dr. White's passing and transition to dwell with the Ancestors, we can still hear his voice, feel his spirit energy, and appreciate the principles he taught us that help us cope with this loss and begin to heal in our broken places.

Healing

One of Joe's most frequently used euphemisms was the concept of *healing in the broken places*. Perhaps then it makes sense to define the construct as we understand it. Healing is a process of recovering and growing from a minor, moderate, or very traumatic event where an individual suffers physical or psychic wound to their person. It is about the elimination of the disease that instigated the discomfort or ailment in the first place. Healing is about the amelioration of the damage one has suffered as a result of intentional or unintentional infliction of pain from another. In the midst of that assault on the human condition, say a cut or wound of some kind, the physical body activates a hemostasis process which begins to address the rupture by seeking to close the wound through clotting. That process can last several days in some cases and is followed by phases outlined as inflammatory, proliferative, and maturation as the injury heals. In a parallel process, people can sustain psychological or social ruptures and injuries as well that represent lacerations that create what West (1996) refers to as mental and emotional scars, ontological wounds, and existential bruises represented by anguish, heartbreak, insult, distress, anxiety, depression, and hurt. Healing in both physical and psychological domains is about becoming whole again and a restoration and return to a normal and healthy level of functioning.

In understanding this notion of normal and healthy functioning, we make an assumption here that there is a natural order in the human condition where individuals are intended to possess and regulate certain qualities and characteristics that adhere to the normal and healthy cycles of growth and development. We also understand and believe, as Fu-Kiau (1991) has taught us through his work, that individuals have a self-healing mechanism which is activated when that human organism or system is threatened or ruptured by people and incidents that are disordered, pathological, or traumatic. In our minds, Joseph L. White understood that there would be broken places in the psychological spaces we all traverse and that in the natural order of our psychological health and wholeness, there would be a need for healing. His concept of resilience and *revitalization* is a most appropriate frame in this regard because Joe White believed in people's capacity to absorb the *blow* to our person, struggle with the adversity, and activate the psychological mechanisms that would lead to a sense of rejuvenation and ultimately the ability to recover from the experience (White, 1984; White & Parham, 1990).

In coming to understand Dr. White as we all did, he was abundantly clear about the fact, as West (1996) would eloquently articulate years later, that in life, there will always be instances of unjustified suffering, unmerited pain, and undeserved harm. Consequently, the question we all must struggle with was not whether misfortune happened but rather how one could sustain some movement and momentum in the process of recovering from those challenges confronting us. In essence, Joe White was teaching and counseling all of us, and others he had contact with, how to adapt to and move beyond disruptive circumstances that were mentally difficult, emotionally painful, physically exhausting, and spiritually disruptive.

In interpreting Dr. White's wisdom, we understand that adaptation is an interesting choice point that provides options when confronted with a life situation or circumstance. In essence, it represents an intellectual, emotional, behavioral, and even spiritual "fork in the road." Instinctually, the human organism is organized to heal ruptures that represent micro-tears in the fabric of our lives. The psychic pain, emotional suffering, and behavioral discombobulation are results of our immediate reactions to situations and circumstances. The process of healing, however, does not start with one's first reaction to circumstances but rather with an ability to absorb the blow to our intellectual, emotional, or behavioral sensibilities; process the cognitive and emotional reactions to the circumstance; sequentially analyze the options and choices available at the time; and then move forward, at whatever pace is most comfortable, in committing to a course of action that remedy the rupture.

And yet, even that response assumes a sense of efficacy and agency to confidently intervene in the task at hand. Thus, when faced with a major or minor challenge or disruption, each individual makes a choice to instinctively and immediately react in the moment and confront the circumstance, sequentially analyze the situation to review all available options and choices before responding, or give in to the circumstance believing that the issue is too overwhelming to manage or change and just live in the emotional or physical pain, defeated by that adversity.

In the Dr. White school of thought we are most familiar with, giving in to a situation was never an option, and reacting without benefiting from first thinking through and analyzing the situation was never the most appropriate posture for one to assume. He always began with an invitation to look inward, process the hurt, and remind oneself of who you were in your identity. He helped you understand that you were loved, capable of managing the situation, and despite the difficulties of the hour, that there were better days ahead as well as joy, laughter, and happiness on the other side of the stormy clouds one was currently experiencing. In those moments where conversations would be intense yet instructive, he would always close with his consistent guidance to "keep the faith." That certainly was a key to healing in the broken places in our lives.

Society's Broken Places

In thinking about "Society's Broken Places," it does not require anyone to look further than the news of the day or track the political system over the past four years to conclude that there is something terribly wrong with the American society. The continued assault on and murder of African American people by police and ordinary citizens alike; torch carrying White supremacists marching through the streets of Charlottesville, Virginia; the targeting and murder of prayer group participants and their pastor in churches; continued discrimination in the application for jobs and opportunities for promotion in the workplace; public policies that have a differential and nefarious impact on Black people's lives; and disproportionate levels of homelessness and hunger are strong indicators that the inequities in Black people's social circumstance are very pronounced. The irony of course is that in the middle of finishing the final draft on this manuscript, the nation just experienced an unprecedented act of domestic terrorism, where a group of President Trump zealots, right-wing Republicans, and other White supremacy groups (Proud Boys, Oath Keepers, QAnon, etc.), unhappy with the results of the 2020 presidential election, engaged in an act of sedition at the site of our nation's capital. Their actions coincided with the scheduled session by the Congress to certify the Electoral College's vote on January 6, 2021. Their violent actions, incited by the sitting president's remarks and encouragement, and emboldened by a Republican political leadership seeking to challenge the legitimate results of the 2020 presidential election, destroyed property, defaced statues, and resulted in personal injury and loss of life. While an analysis of the scandalous behaviors of those involved is beyond the scope of this chapter, the incidents of January 6, 2021 do illustrate that the system of democracy has some cracks and fissures in it and that the need for our nation to heal in many broken places is urgent and profound.

Parham, T. (2021) used the incident at the Capitol to frame a different set of questions that speak more directly to the focus of this chapter. In using Frederick Douglas' 1852 address on what the *July 4th* celebration really meant to the American slaves, Parham asked a similar set of queries about what the participation in the rituals of electoral democracy really held for African Americans and other people of color. The realities of life in Black America are that there is a historic absence of reciprocal exchange, where people who invest in and support the growth and development of an institution or family expect there to be some privilege and courtesy extended to them. Despite having helped build this nation with forced and unforced labor, fight in global and regional wars and conflicts to defend American democracy, served in federal, state, and local law enforcement agencies that protect the public interests, and practiced good citizenship by following the social expectation of trying to educate oneself, support law and order, embrace religiosity as a guidepost for a purpose-driven life, and live honest and decent lives, African American people are still denied an equal opportunity to full participation and equality in the American society. Indeed, participation in the electoral process, and having a say in how the affairs of the world are managed, is a reasonable expectation for those who cast their ballots each Election Day. And yet, what do the rituals this nation celebrates each election cycle with tabulating state and local precinct election results, counting electoral college votes, congressional certifications, and inauguration celebrations really mean to Black people if the policies and practices in the nation continue to be conducted with scandalous inconsistency? This condition represents a broken place in the lives of African American people and evidence of a serious structural defect in the fabric of society.

Voices of the people crying out for relief from the systems of oppression all over this nation that infect their daily lives bear witness to their suffering and misery. Dyson's (2017) text titled *Tears We Cannot Stop: My Sermon to White America* provides an intellectually riveting account of the way race relations in this nation have become more divisive and splintered. He argues that progress in creating a more just and equitable society is inhibited by a fundamental denial about racism in America and how the grievances of the Black, poor, dispossessed, and disinherited peoples of this nation are discounted or otherwise ignored. Acho (2020), in his efforts to broker "uncomfortable Conversations" in his new book, writes about the systemic racism that permeates the fabric of society's institutions, including housing, schooling, and criminal justice. While what is wrong has been wrong for some time, the events over the past several years have brought to light the inequities that exist in the American society that include disparities in health care, education, homelessness, voting rights and state government practices, police brutality and murdering Black lives, and criminal justice, just to name a few.

One of the more visible examples of oppression's residual impact occurred in 2008, some 13 years ago, during the campaign of then Senator Obama. In the 2008 spring and fall seasons, he was running for president of the United States. While living in Chicago, he was a member and attended Trinity United Church of Christ, which at the time was pastored by Rev. Jeremiah Wright. Wright, whose vociferous orations blended Christianity and liberation theology, had occasionally been critical about U.S. policy in its domestic and foreign affairs. When ABC News decided to air excerpts of Rev. Wright's speeches into an edited couple of minute video thread, those excerpts were used by Obama's political competition and other news agencies to try and derail his campaign's momentum. In response to the controversy, Candidate Obama delivered a consequential address from Philadelphia, explaining his position as a then candidate.

While Obama was clear about distancing himself from Rev. Wright's remarks, he took the occasion to contextualize the sentiments expressed in those church sermons. He tried to assist people, who viewed and listened to his Philadelphia speech, in understanding how a person of Jeremiah Wright's stature and service record could still harbor the residuals of coping with a lifetime of oppression while also bearing witness to the subjugation and mistreatment of others (Obama, 2020). The anger, hurt, pain, resentment, and disappointment in America's incongruence that he expressed represent the cracks or fissures in the emotional and intellectual armor that Rev. Wright and others bolster their sense of self with. And yet, even in the adjustments we all make to life's adversities, there is no doubt that for many people in this nation, especially African American and other people of color, there is a need to heal in those broken places.

Broken places can be described here as differences in disadvantaged social groups such as the poor, racial/ethnic minorities, women, and other groups who have persistently experienced social disadvantage or discrimination and experienced worse or poor treatment and access to resources to help manage their life circumstances. According to the Medicare Advocacy Group, "when systemic barriers to good health are avoidable yet still remain, they are often referred to as 'health inequities.'" That is a broken place. Other "Broken Places" include the criminal justice system where there is a disproportionate number of African American males and females incarcerated, some receiving sentences much longer than their Caucasian counterparts for the same crime. If we examine the news and see the senseless killings of Breonna Taylor, George Floyd, Tamir Rice, and others by law enforcement officials, with no criminal charges being filed against any of the officers involved, it is a "broken place" in the society's system of justice that claims to provide and guarantee equal protection under the law.

We also see broken places in education. When children in affluent areas like Beverly Hills, California, receive the newest textbooks that adequately prepare them to take the standardized test in California (CST) but children in South Central Los Angeles are afforded only secondhand or outdated books, because funding to their respective neighborhoods is based on an economic standard of property value and related tax base, gross levels of inequality are evident. Yet, when both groups are required to take the same standardized tests that measure their supposed readiness to manage the rigors of a college or university education, with scores impacting the ability to attend a higher education institution, it is a "broken place." Broken too are the systems of pedagogy, instructional methodology, and administrative practices that treat Black and other children of color differently as a result of their race. Black students have more restricted access to gifted educational opportunities, receive skewed and biased advising related to college preparation, have more discipline imposed for minor offenses when compared to their White peers, and are subjected to diminished expectations regarding their academic performance because of an unfavorable appraisal of their intellectual capability.

Beyond these systemic descriptions of those spaces in need of repair, it is equally important to highlight the interpersonal domains that reside in the cognitive, affective, behavioral, and spiritual spaces that represent the core of our personality and identity. Personality in this regard is a complex set of traits or attributes that define a person's uniqueness. Relatedly, our identity is a sum total of characteristics that describes the person we believe ourselves to be, or aspire to become, which includes a portrait of what we consider to be our nature, our essence, and our character. Those characteristics we adopt are colored and shaped by the demographics we represent, the developmental experiences we are involved in and/or exposed to, the socialization and validation we are given from primary caregivers and networks of community friends, how significant others in our lives respond to and affirm our humanity, and how the world outside of our immediate family of caregivers reacts to the person we believe ourselves to be. The complex interplay of these factors, in turn, helps us make meaning out of situations, interrogate attributions about why things are the way they are, ascribe certain aspects of those experiences to our own identity, and influence how we interact with and react to other people and situational circumstances we encounter.

Externally, much of the makeup of these "broken places" has been the direct result of one or more of the many isms (racism, sexism, classism) that have existed in this country since its inception. The history of slavery, women's suffrage, and the division of wealth in this nation have all contributed to the mindset of many that is the anchor for these antiquated systems. While what is wrong has been wrong for some time, the events over the past several years have brought to light other inequities that exist in U.S. society that include disparities in health care, education, and criminal justice that we describe above, just to name a few. Given the illumination of the "isms," and additional discriminatory policies and practices that govern us or that are manipulated to create these oppressive systems, it is now clear that there are a number of elements that need to be addressed if we are to manage change in our lifetime. Brilliant scholars, Henry Louis Gates Jr., and Cornell West remind us that "Race differences and class differentials have been ground together in this country in a crucible of misery and squalor in such a way that few of us know where one stops and the other begins" (Gates & West, 1996).

In a similar way, and decades before, W.E.B. Dubois articulated "the problem of the Twentieth Century as the problem of the color line" (1996). While many members of the White community do not see it as a problem, it is because their perception has been clouded for years, with miseducation about what the world outside of their walled castles really is for those who live their lives at the margins of society. While this may have been the case of a covert system of oppression in the past, what we would pose is our witnessing of a dying way of life. It has been suggested that the wealthy have nothing left to sustain the deception that has been their clothing for centuries. America cannot and should not return to the old ways, and yet change from a lengthy and sordid history is difficult, particularly if it is unwanted or perceived as not possible.

What is true is that we can affect change if we want to. We remember several lectures and keynote addresses given by Dr. White in which content was very visionary. What made it so, unlike other keynotes, was the persona that was Dr. White. He believed in keeping it real. He told you the truth, at least as he saw it, but did it in a way that whether you agreed or not, you had nothing but respect for him and what he shared. Here was a man who, in mentoring countless numbers of students, never asked for anything in return, except to do for someone (or others) what he did for you. He understood that there would be people who did not agree with him and his perspective about any given topic, but that did not diminish their person. He reminded us all that different does not mean deficient, but it just meant different. He was also very clear that listening to folks who may see or experience life differently was a good way to get to know them. We believe developing that skill is an effective strategy for change.

Even as we briefly highlight some of society's broken places, we are very cognizant of the fact that progress has been made in the years since we were children and young adults. No question about it. Advances in technology, transportation, communications and media, health care, athletics, space exploration, scientific discoveries, political appointments to high offices, etc. are a testament to the growth and development of society. We are also aware that the level of resistance to continued progress and empowerment of a people is equally pronounced and more sophisticated than was historically the case. Even as we author this chapter, we are cognizant of the fact that:

- Poverty is still the norm for too many of our nation's children.
- Racism is still an infectious disease on the health of this nation and a stain on this experiment we call democracy.
- Violence against Black, Brown, and poor people and women continues unabated in the cities and suburbs of our country.
- Women continue to receive less pay for equal work.
- Discrimination against the physically challenged and others who are LGBTQ is still a challenge we as a society have yet to overcome.
- Education is still unequal at K-12 levels, and too many colleges and universities in this nation contribute to climates where higher education is treated as a privilege of the few rather than a fundamental right of the many.
- We have fitness machines to help us build more muscular and finely toned bodies, yet we have no machines to help us better love one another across demographic boundaries or create more enlightened levels of compassion and sensitivity to people whose lives are lived at the margins of society.

In essence, much has changed and very little has changed in our lifetime. So, the struggle continues, and daily news and life experiences continue to expose and reveal the ruptures in the fabric of society.

Practical Strategies for Leaders and Change Makers

In contemplating and reflecting on strategies for leaders and change makers to navigate the terrain of helping individuals and organizations heal in the broken places, we would offer the following recommendations.

First, we believe that it is difficult if not impossible for leaders and change makers to initiate the healing process if individuals, institutions, and agencies continue to linger in a climate of denial. The first premise we would suggest for healing in society's broken places and spaces is to assess the desire for change. Dr. White often referred to that process as sequential analysis where one literally analyzes the circumstance and assesses if the climate is right for change, or an individual or organization is committed to stagnation and the status quo. If the recognition of broken places and the commitment to change is not something that is seen as beneficial, then no amount of effort will be as impactful when compared to a situation or circumstance being perceived as a growth step toward a continued healing, recovery, and development.

We are also reminded here that one of the most challenging tasks an individual will face is related to what Parham, T (1996) and Nobles (1986) before him refer to as "conceptual incarceration." According to Nobles (1986), it represents one domain of the broader construct referred to as "scientific colonialism" or the political control of knowledge. The term speaks to the observation that a person's thinking is anchored in a distorted or culturally incongruent worldview that results in an extremely restricted view of their person and the circumstances they manage and confront daily. Understanding that construct is important here because if an individual or institution is afflicted with a conceptually incarcerated mindset, where self-awareness is limited, perceptions of reality are skewed or distorted, and denial of particular individual or social conditions is commonplace, then the ability to heal in whatever broken place that individual or institution may be experiencing is inhibited. Consequently, the biggest challenge that must be addressed beyond the circumstance people and institutions face is the need for mental liberation and finding ways to unlock and release the shackles of conceptual incarceration.

To reach the kind of equitable positions we talk about, demonstrate, and pray for, it is required for us to take the shackles off of our minds and the blinders off our eyes to see the frailties and vulnerabilities that have impacted individuals and institutions and extend empathy and compassion to those who bear the suffering. Seeing clearly is the first step in any individual's transformational journey (Williams, 2004). Dr. King shared that "People struggling from the depths of society have not been equipped with the knowledge of the science of social change. Only when they break out of the fog of self-denigration can they begin to discover the forms of action that influence events" (King, 1968). In essence, we must also recognize and prioritize, with certain understanding, that changes are not group specific but are reciprocal and will be required by all in order to realize the fullest expression of its substance.

Second, healing from whatever individual or systemic breaks impact our individual or organizational lives will require some measure of love and a capacity to forgive. A wounded spirit feels the pain and sorrow that is a constant reminder of promises unkept, a hurt that was inflicted, and a disappointment realized. And yet, leaders and change makers will need to understand, as Dr. King so eloquently expressed, that "darkness cannot drive out darkness, only light can do that. Hate cannot drive out hate, only love can do that." The energy required to hold on to the pain and setback robs individuals of their ability to transcend their pain and move to a different plateau of the emotional vitality Joe White referenced in his classroom lectures and books. Thus, while individual and institutional memory are important elements in reinforcing the protective factors that support individual and institutional survival, the capacity to forgive and release the tension, anxiety, and pain, and replace them with amnesty, absolution, and grace (favor and goodwill), is a necessary and requisite step in the healing process.

Third, healing in those broken places, where institutional and systemic factors are the point of concern, will require a fundamental shift in how our governments, cities, states, and nation define progress. What we are suggesting is that the milestone markers of real and substantive change be altered from simplistic markers of incremental progress to a more authentic marker of true equality. For example, no longer are people simply satisfied with mere token efforts to desegregate institutions, organizations, policies, or population demographics. What people are demanding is real change where the power to define, influence, and control outcomes is shared among all people involved rather than a few individuals isolated in their privilege or leadership position. In this way, leaders and change makers will need to become consummate risk takers, learning to take three types of risk. There are mental risks, where one learns to think outside of the box. There are verbal risks, where one offers ideas and asserts opinions that push the boundaries of what is considered the status quo. Lastly, there are behavioral risks where an individual commits him/herself to do something unconventional as a way of addressing the fracture of life's broken places.

Fourth, leaders and change makers will need to help individuals learn to "contextualize struggle," as they help them heal. Context in this regard is about assessing and chronicling the situational variables that may have influenced a prior outcome in a different circumstance and then comparing that to one you may be encountering in the moment. Dr. White was a firm believer in "the value of direct experience" (White & Parham, 1990). That belief, however, extended both to a person's lived encounters with an experience and reference to a past historical event that helped reframe the breadth and depth of the situation one found themselves managing in the moment. For example, on the walls of Thomas' offices, he keeps a picture of the Ancestors and slave dungeons in the castles at El Mina and Cape Coast in Ghana, West Africa. The images taken by Dr. Parham while on a trip to Ghana in 2000 with the national Association of Black Psychologists remind him, and all of us, about the horrors of slavery and the suffering, human degradation, and brutality African descent people suffered at the hands of their captors. And yet, the sacrifices made by that generation of Ancestors and elders allowed current generations to more fully engage the world they live in today. Consequently, when one feels that they have been disrespected, disillusioned, hurt or insulted, or suffered indignity (ranging from a microaggression, micro-assault, or micro-invalidation, all the way to a traumatic experience with racism, sexism, etc.), at the hands of another, very intense emotional reactions are a likely result. Contextualizing struggle in that regard allows leaders and change makers to facilitate a more moderate and functional response, especially when the current situation is compared to historical precedent. Helping an individual or organization frame their experience within the broader portrait of life's realities and analogous circumstances can be a useful strategy in helping to aid and even ease the challenges being ad-dressed in the moment. Indeed, Dr. White would constantly remind us all the pain, struggle, and tragedy were just a part of "paying one's dues," and the healing in those broken places was more than possible (White, 1984). Care must be taken however to avoid dismissing an individual or institution's intellectual and emotional space or pain as unimportant or insignificant. Everyone's experiences are important to them, even as leaders and change makers help them place their observations, encoun-ters, involvements, and the resulting impact in context.

Fifth, another element of Dr. White's wisdom-teachings was the need to learn to assess how much change and movement an environment would tolerate. In this regard, whether one is enrolling in and commenc-ing a new graduate school program, beginning a new job or position in an institution or corporation, or engaging in civic activity with a local, state, or federal government agency, it is not uncommon to identify elements of incongruence between stated mission and goals and what is actually practiced. Not surprisingly, it is a normal outcome to question individual or organizational needs for change. The changes people often insist need to be made may be evidence of broken places within that individual's or organization's structure, policies, and/or practices. The challenge here of course is that not all people view life from the same lens, and some may not perceive there to be a problem at all. It is also likely that people have an investment in the way things are organized and are managed. Con-sequently, any suggestions for change may not be perceived as simply a recommendation but rather an implicit assault on the efforts that others engaged in to build and construct what some are not critiquing. Leaders and change makers will need to be aware of this fact and assist people and organizations in first assessing a readiness or willingness to change and heal and a tolerance for managing the growth opportunity that may be more latent than visible to those invested in the status quo.

Sixth, as leaders and change makers work with people who are committed to serving others and promoting opportunities to heal in the broken places of life, they will need to keep an eye on how much people are willing to sacrifice for that endeavor. Advancing the notion of healing, particularly in those situations when the need is not recognized or called for, often requires an individual to risk stepping out on a proverbial limb. The risk required to provide observation, offer feedback, or critique, or sound the alarm that something may be terribly wrong and needs healing, brings with it reactions from individuals and institutions. In some cases, the reactions represent an acceptance of the observation and perhaps even a willingness to further interrogate what is perceived as incongruent, misaligned, or wrong. In other respects, such efforts may instigate instances of defensiveness, resistance, and counterattack, where the individual raising the observations now becomes the subject of scrutiny. At risk, of course, are things like receiving personal critique, other individuals and organizations now being more uncomfortable with one's presence, a loss of status within an organization or among one's social network, or maybe a denial of opportunities to grow within that system because that individual may be regarded as anti-collegial or not a team player. Understand here that the challenge is not simply individual but also systemic. Organizations value harmony, compliance with their cultural ethos, and a stable momentum that keeps the organization moving consistently toward meeting its objectives. Thus, anything that is believed to threaten or otherwise disrupt that continuity is not always received in a positive light. Not surprisingly, there may be risks. Conversely, if the organization is already experiencing discord within its people, policies, and practices, and is now searching for answers to healing whatever breach may have been exposed, it may be more receptive to a process of analysis, feedback, and recommendations. They will however still need to explore the risk/reward of what such efforts may mean to the organization as a whole. In some circumstances, these risks and consequences are real; in other respects, the risks may be more imagined, as the individual or organization being referenced may be extremely receptive and quite desirous of the feedback being provided. Consequently, leaders and change makers will need to help individuals and organizations seek answers to the query and examine at a deep-structure level what are they prepared to sacrifice in order to instigate a process of healing in a place believed to be broken.

Seventh, we believe that it is important to lead with love and not fear. Dr. White's concept of emotional vitality and expressiveness invites leaders and change makers to consider that being emotionally expressive with those who are in pain and in need of healing in their broken places is an important strategy. Contrary to traditional psychology's notion of remaining a detached objective outsider, authentic connectedness and the expression of genuine caring in the spirit of love leadership seem like a more potent antidote. Reinforcing Dr. White's notion of emotional vitality, Bryant (2009) reminds us about what he calls the laws of love leadership. Included among that list are the beliefs that *fear fails, loss and vulnerability identify hidden strengths and instigates power*, and that *giving is getting*. Whether you are addressing an individual or institutional entity, many people's narratives are skewed in the domain of being fear based. Not only does that posture or perspective evoke negative energy, but it also contributes to a sense of powerlessness that gets in the way of healing. Leading with love also invites the exposure of vulnerability. Expressing vulnerability creates an atmosphere of universality in helping others know that they are not alone in their pain or struggles. Reciprocally, sharing vulnerability invites others to witness and learn from a leader's experience of how they too overcame adversity on their way to healing in whatever broken places appeared in their lives. Leaders and change makers will need to understand that the vulnerability required in the process of healing is related to one's intellectual and emotional fortitude. Strength, however, is not measured in moments of comfort and convenience but rather is found in the depth of one's discomfort and the ability, despite that pain, hurt, or anger, to generate and sustain movement and momentum toward healing. Indeed, on the continuum of life, represented by polarities of pleasure, good fortune, hopefulness, and contentment, on one side, and unhappiness, depression, sorrow, and despair, on the other, an individual or organization will never find out how strong it can be until its moment of greatest vulnerability.

Finally, leaders and change makers will need to be, and help others they inspire to be, authentic truth tellers about the realities that impact people's lives. Dr. White referred to this as "keep'in it real" (White, 1984; White & Parham, 1990). Realness in this regard allows people to separate out those factors that are systemic and more difficult to control, from those that are individually derived and can be addressed with intentional strategies within the capacity of that person or organization. We have found that in the context of human and organizational authenticity, there is often a gap between the real self and the aspirational self that seeks a greater degree of perfectibility. Obviously, we all recognize that beyond the CREATOR, no individual, system, or organization is perfect, without flaws, or completely beyond improvement. Those imperfections, flaws, and defects are the personal behaviors, institutional policies, or situational variables that often create the fractures and fissures in our lives we all experience as broken places. Leaders and change makers, in their efforts to render meaningful and consequential impact to the people and causes they touch, will do well to remember that. Being a messenger of healing, hope, and optimism must first engender trust and credibility from the individuals and organizations one seeks to help heal. If people trust the messenger and believe the message to be reliable and credible because it is anchored in authentic observations that correspond to people's perceptions of their reality, then the energy invested in the recovery and healing process will not be derailed or contaminated by elements of distrust, irrelevance, or a lack of credibility.

Closing Thoughts

Interestingly, Dr. White (1984) and White and Parham, (1990) asserted, and we would affirm, that some of the most authentic truth tellers can be found among the artists and entertainers, writers and poets, and public intellectuals of their day, who utilize their craft and platform to lay bare the inconsistent, gut-wrenching, and often horrific realities people experience. Remembering those texts, and the wisdom within those pages Dr. White authored and co-authored, provides a platform from which to launch a few closing notes to this chapter. Healing in the broken places is an endeavor worth the time it takes to do the difficult work. The amount of pain, hurt, disappointment, anger, disillusionment, distrust, and disgust in our nation could fill an ocean. Thus, genuine healing must first begin with an acknowledgment that the pain is real and healing is necessary.

We are clear that oppression is caused by individual and systemic behaviors. Racism, sexism, homophobia, discrimination, Islamophobia, etc. are all instigated by individuals and their behaviors. The murder of Black and Brown bodies by law enforcement personnel, the differential and discriminatory treatment children of color receive from teachers in schools and professors in colleges and universities, the economic policies and practices that allow poverty to go unaddressed, the biased and inadequate care people receive in the health care system based on their demographics, the unequal justice people of color receive in the courts, and the efforts to suppress the vote of entire segments of the nation's population are all challenges our local communities and the entire nation will need to overcome. Authentic truth telling about our condition as a people and a nation brokers a more honest appraisal about both individual and systemic situations that then invite genuine and reliable reflection from individuals, organizations, and institutions. Being genuine and honest with people affirms and validates their reality that something is terribly wrong in their life situation that may or may not be related to their own behaviors. Truth telling lets people know that they are not delusional when it comes to their experiences with inequity and unfairness and that the oppression they feel is real. Being real helps individuals and institutions come to terms with the difference between actual facts versus imaginary fictitiousness. Indeed, for many people, perception is reality, and their ability to heal in those broken places requires an honest and legitimate appraisal of what the challenge that lay before them is and an articulation of those forces and resources that can be brought to bear in achieving some resolution.

Leaders and change makers, in the spirit of Dr. Joseph White, must learn to avoid retreating from the verifiable facts about the night side of people's life experiences while also offering a narrative that sees hope on the horizon, progress in the places where stagnation reigned, and belief in people and system's ability to change and transform into a more whole, healthy, and healing place. Perhaps Gorman (2021) best captured these sentiments in her captivating recitation of a poem for the Biden-Harris Presidential Inauguration titled *The Hill We Climb*. In her nearly five-minute oration, she began by asking the question of "where can we find light in the never ending shade," acknowledging the challenges of oppression and discrimination that America and her people had struggled through and referenced the assault of people's humanity and our nation's democracy witnessed by all just two weeks earlier (Gorman, 2021). And yet, the eyes and heart of a 22-year-old offered a hopeful and optimistic pathway forward for our nation's healing in her closing refrain. She closed her poetic address with the following words:

> *When day comes we step out of the shade, aflame and unafraid, the new dawn blooms as we free it. For there is always light, if only we're brave enough to see it. If only we're brave enough to be it.*
>
> (Gorman, 2021)

Those sentiments speak with an uncompromising clarity about the challenges of our day and echo precisely what Dr. White wrote and spoke about regarding the need to heal in the broken places. For broken places are an inevitable part of life's journey as we synthesize the sunshine and storms that characterize our experiences. But so too is the human capacity to heal the rupture and extend the splendor, for such is the nature and essence of the human character we have within us, if only we take time to see it and be it.

Discussion Questions

1   As a mental health provider, you are engaged in the art of healing. What does healing mean to you, and how would you recognize it in an individual you were treating?
2   How do you define "broken places," and how do those definitions vary across systemic and individual dimensions?
3   What do you see as the broken places that exist in individual and societal domains of our lives?
4   In your study of the principles of an African American psychology, what cultural elements (mores, values, customs, traditions) of that

worldview best align with the strategies you might employ in facilitating change in the world?

5   If "keeping it real" and being a truth teller are essential for leaders
and change makers in facilitating healing in the broken places of our
lives, what inhibits you from providing more open and honest feedback to others?

6   If artists, entertainers, and athletes are some of the most authentic
truth tellers, what song, poem, or example resonates with you in explaining the challenges we face as a society?

7   What are you most optimistic about as the future shines through the
storms of life with rays of hope, possibility, and healing?

References

Acho, E. (2020). *Uncomfortable Conversations With a Black Man*. New York:
Flatiron Books.

Akbar, N. (1992). *Chains and Images of Psychological Slavery*. Tallahassee, FL:
Mind Productions.

Bryant, J. H. (2009). *Love Leadership: The New Way to Lead in a Fear Based
World*. San Francisco, CA: Jossey-Bass.

Du Bois, W. E. B. (1968). *The Souls of Black Folk*. Mineola, NY: Dover Publications Inc.

Dyson, M. E. (2017). *Tears We Cannot Stop: My Sermon to White America*. New
York: St. Martin's Press.

Fu-Kiau, K. K. (1991). *Self-Healing Power and Therapy: Old Teachings from
Africa*. New York: Vantage Books.

Gates, H. L. Jr., & West, C. (1996). *The Future of the Race*. New York: Vintage
Publications.

Gorman, A. (2021). *The Hill We Climb*. [Unpublished poem] Inauguration of
President Joseph Biden, Washington, DC.

Guthrie, R. V. (1976). *Even the Rat Was White: A Historical View of Psychology*.
New York: Harper and Rowe.

Ivey, A., D'Andrea, M., Bradford-Ivey, M., & Simek-Morgan, L. (2002). *Theories
of Counseling and Psychotherapy: A Multicultural Perspective* (5th Ed). Boston,
MA: Allyn & Bacon.

Jones, R. L. (1972). *Black Psychology*. New York: Harper & Rowe.

Jones, R. L. (1980). *Black Psychology* (2nd Ed). New York: Harper & Rowe.

King, M. L., Jr. (1968). *Where Do We Go from Here, Chaos or Community?* Boston, MA: Beacon Press.

Nobles, W. W. (1986). *African Psychology: Towards Its Reclamation, Reascension,
and Revitalization*. Oakland, CA: The Black Family Institute.

Obama, B. H. (2020). *A Promised Land*. New York: Crown Publishing.

Parham, T. A. (1996). *Passport to the Future Program*. [Unpublished curriculum
developed for the 100 Black Men of Orange County Rites of Passage program].

Parham, T. A. (2021). *Teachable Moments Regarding the Nation's Culture: Is It
Time for Higher Education Institutions to Help Place Genuine Equality Front
and Center in Our National Discourse*. Los Angeles Sentinel Newspaper.

Retrieved from. TEACHABLE MOMENTS REGARDING THE NATION'S CULTURE: IS IT TIME FOR HIGHER EDUCATION INSTITUTIONS TO HELP PLACE GENUINE EQUALITY FRONT AND CENTER IN OUR NATIONAL DISCOURSE? – Los Angeles Sentinel | Los Angeles Sentinel | Black News (lasentinel.net).

Parham, T. A., Ajamu, A., & White, J. L. (2011). *The Psychology of Blacks: Centering Our Perspective in The African Consciousness* (4th Ed). Upper Saddle River, NJ: Prentice Hall.

Sue, D. W. (1981). *Counseling the Culturally Different.* New York: John Wiley & Sons.

Sue, D. W., & Sue, D. (1990). *Counseling the Culturally Different* (2nd Ed). New York: John Wiley & Sons.

Sue, D. W., & Sue, D. (2003). *Counseling the Culturally Diverse* (3rd Ed). New York: John Wiley & Sons

West, C. (August, 1996). *The Duality of Spirituality.* [Address] Chicago, IL: National Convention of the Association of Black Psychologists.

White, J. L. (1984). *The Psychology of Blacks: An Afro-American Perspective* (1st Ed). Englewood Cliffs, NJ: Prentice Hall.

White, J. L. (1970). Towards a Black Psychology. *Ebony Magazine*, 25, 44–53.

White, J. L. (1972). Towards a Black Psychology. In R. L. Jones (Ed) *Black Psychology*, pp. 43–50. New York: Harper & Row.

White, J. L., & Parham, T. A.,(1990). *The Psychology of Blacks: An African American Perspective* (2nd Ed). Englewood Cliffs, NJ: Prentice Hall.

White, J. L., & Parham, T. A. (2015). *Dr. Thomas Parham & Dr. Joseph White – Meeting Parham.* University of California Irvine Archives. Retrieved from Dr. Thomas Parham & Dr. Joseph L White & - Meeting Parham – YouTube.

Williams, J. (2004). *My Soul Looks Back in Wonder: Voices of the Civil Rights Movement.* New York: Sterling Publishing.

8 Creating Organizational Tracks

The Freedom Train Forging New Paths

Nita Tewari

Figure 8.1 Image of Nita Tewari and Joseph L. White. Provided by and used with permission of Nita Tewari (2022).

DOI: 10.4324/9781003132899-11

First-Person Narrative

I have had many profound mentee experiences in my 30-year relationship spanning from 1990 to 2017 with Dr. Joseph L. White. As a 20-year-old community college transfer student to the University of California, Irvine (UCI), one particular conversation stood out in our mentoring relationship which began soon after completing Dr. White's undergraduate UCI Adolescent Psychology in American Society course. Predictably, mentoring time with "Joe" began with his "business first, then we'll socialize" conversational style sprinkled with "critical Joe teaching moments." In my early years while walking on campus at UCI's ring road as a psychology major, Dr. White asked me an especially poignant question: "What does it mean for you to be an Indian American female living in America?" Prior to Dr. White asking, I had not thought about this question. He challenged me to think about what it meant to be an Indian American woman born in Southern Californian in 1970. Dr. White listened carefully and looked at me through his glasses, and sometimes over his glasses. I shared my frustration about having to explain where I was from and who I was to the white people around me. And how my brown skin and dark hair did not match up with their racial expectations (i.e., I was not who they usually thought would have these physical characteristics).

I believe that he understood that I knew who I was, and he judged that from my strong reaction, tinged with both anger and sadness, that he should respond with empathy, truth, and conviction. Dr. White told me:

> Don't let white folks or anyone else tell you who you are, what your identity is. You define what it means to be Indian. If you don't, white folks and others will. And they aren't going know what they're talking about either because they don't know what it's like to be Indian American growing up in the United States. So, you need to be the one talking about your experiences as an Asian American, a South Asian American and an Indian American woman. All the things you just told me, that's what you need to write about and practice. In the process, you gotta' find folks and create your own support system that understands the psychological experiences of your people.

Dr. White also touched upon his own experiences of being African American and dealing with racism, as well as examples of how other People of Color navigated majority white spaces.

No one had ever spoken to me so candidly about race and color in America. He discussed the importance of pursuing higher education as a Woman of Color. But he also went further to share his vision of my potential future. He provided a road map for how to successfully pursue a major in psychology that might lead to graduate school. He envisioned me having a fruitful career where I might develop a private practice, become published, and make an impact in my community. Dr. White's confidence in me set the stage for my further self-reflection and helped me to develop my vision for the future. This eventually led to my acceptance into a counseling psychology doctoral program.

During my time as a graduate student, I spoke regularly with Dr. White. Our conversations became an informal education on the evolution of ethnic studies, the critique of psychology as a discipline, its history, and how this led to mainstream psychological organizations falling short in providing culturally relevant support for People of Color. Over time, I learned that these conversations were not random but rather that Dr. White was intentional in his mentorship. He thought deeply about how to best guide his mentees and impart wisdom unique to each individual and their strengths. He was a master of providing developmentally appropriate mentoring that laid the groundwork for his mentees' personal and professional growth.

In this chapter, I describe how Dr. White's question and subsequent conversations served as a foundation to build a formal support structure that normalized and validated cultural, ethnic, and racial differences of my ethnic group in America. More specifically, I share how I formed a networking association and then later formalized a divisional structure that organized individuals dedicated to furthering research and practice on South Asian mental health. Throughout the chapter, I identify how Dr. White's teachings in his quoted words can help create "something from nothing" by leveraging networks and working with existing organizations to establish support structures and "taking talk to the next level."

Analysis of Narrative

Dr. White's mentoring occurred at any given time whether it was one-on-one time, during a hallway conversation, or while "holding court" (i.e., gathering peers and mentees) in a hotel bar at a psychology conference. His informal, strategic mentoring style was his all-inclusive way of connecting on a personal level while providing developmentally specific academic and professional guidance. Key to Dr. White's mentoring were asking critical questions, "planting seeds" (helping you consider an idea you had not previously thought about), and "devising plans for the future" (encouraging you to develop intentional and strategic professional goals for your life).

He was clear that success could not happen alone and that I would need to learn about existing support systems (e.g., graduate students, professors, solo practitioners, key community advocates, and administrators in non-psychology departments) and network with them. Most importantly, he believed in what he called the "shake and bake." Dr. White explained that being open and flexible, meeting new people, showing initiative, and taking chances could help ensure that one always landed on their feet.

He emphasized adaptability when attempting to seize a moment and taking risks. Dr. White especially encouraged those he mentored to attend as many local and national conferences as possible, whether it was for the purpose of finding others with shared experiences or help build new "Freedom Train tracks" for other "Freedom Train riders."

In order to build insight into how to develop this type of organization, Dr. White walked me through how the Association of Black Psychologists (ABPsi) evolved from the 1960s civil rights movement. He explained how ABPsi was established to address the concerns of Black psychologists who were systematically ignored by the American Psychological Association (APA) as they joined Black psychiatrists and other mental health professionals as they attempted to address the harm that APA and other mental health organizations did to Black communities. Dr. White told me about how he and others spread the word about forming a Black psychology organization, how they made flyers, used open hallway space to meet, took pictures of attendees who came to the gathering for documentation, and contacted individuals in the media to write a story about the formation of ABPsi. This set the scene for other ethnic and racial psychological organizations to follow, as well as APA divisions that focused on the needs of marginalized communities (i.e., the Society for the Psychological Study of Culture, Ethnicity and Race, Division 45).

Given the struggles of APA, an organization that continues to work toward embracing diversity, but has yet to meet the mark in terms of training and graduate curriculum, I feel fortunate to have been influenced by Dr. White's experiences. He explained the importance of racial and ethnic awareness, the need to develop cultural competency, and the critical focus on clients attempting to take on an emic (i.e., insider) viewpoint rather than accepting an etic (i.e., outsider) perspective when assessing and treating individuals with different worldviews. Dr. White clearly described the steps by sharing his own experiences and how others started with informal support, organized groups, learned who the players were, developed allies, and formalized systemic changes. His ability to describe details and talk about the big picture provided me with a road map guide on how to align academic, political, and educational agendas that supported causes in psychology or underrepresented individuals whether they were students, clients, or patients.

Identifying the Need

As a new transfer student at UC Irvine, Dr. White gave me a clear picture of how to identify areas in psychology where gaps existed by asking thought-provoking questions to people with open minds. My awareness of the absence of South Asian American voices in psychology began with him asking about my opinions and experiences. He started by asking me what it was like to be an Indian American woman living in the United

States. Sharing my observations and thinking critically about what existed and what was absent in the field of psychology was an eye-opening experience for me. Dr. White taught me that before creating change in a system, one must identify the need based upon the track record and history of the institutions involved.

Dr. White encouraged his mentees to seize opportunities as they related to serving the needs of underrepresented people. As I pursued my major in psychology, I began to notice that the experiences of South Asians and Asian Americans were not discussed in my required undergraduate psychology courses and were absent from the psychological literature. By the end of my educational training, the scarcity of information pertaining to the clinical needs and research on Asian Americans, South Asian Americans, and Indian Americans served as my inspiration to help build infrastructure with the intention of creating spaces for my communities within the field of psychology.

Broadening Your Knowledge Base

Dr. White encouraged broadening knowledge, which included attending professional conferences to learn what others in the field were presenting nationally, regionally, or locally outside of daily networks. In 1993, when applying to graduate school, Dr. White encouraged me to attend my first APA and Asian American Psychological Association (AAPA) conventions with other students. His goal for my attendance was to learn what psychologists talk about, what they teach and what psychological organizations do and to observe who the "players, movers and shakers" were in the field. While at the convention, before and after program symposiums, Dr. White methodically introduced me to division leaders, professors, committee members, and students and invited other students to accompany him at social hours to meet like-minded people and those with new ideas. Most importantly, he introduced us to colleagues who had power, influence, experience, and a willingness to be inclusive to the next generation of psychologists.

Dr. White emphasized the importance of meeting people in a variety of disciplines across the nation, as those from the West Coast had different life perspectives and experiences than those from the Midwest and East Coast. His dedication to introducing mentees to his peers and colleagues nationally was a deliberate method to help broaden our experiences. Through these introductions, I became more comfortable interacting outside of my local university context and was able to discuss topics that were absent from the curriculum of my degree program.

I remember at one such APA convention where I was thrilled to have an in-depth discussion with a Native American colleague, specifically regarding my frustration about how Indigenous people were racially labeled as Indians by white people. I shared with my Native American colleague that I continuously felt unseen due to the inherent racism of confusing two different cultural groups (i.e., Indigenous Peoples in the Americas and South Asians from India) as "Indian" and the stereotyping of what an "Indian" was believed to look like. Interestingly, my colleague had no idea that Asian Indian Americans struggled with the use of the word "Indian" because they assumed that most Americans believed that the general term "Indian" was referring to Native Americans.

Although there is variation among South Asian Indians in self-labeling, most South Asian Indians ethnically identify as Indians, describe themselves by region (e.g., Punjabi), or use the term "South Asian" to culturally describe themselves. Geographically, since India is in the continent of Asia, Indians have also used the term "Asian Indian" to distinguish themselves racially and ethnically from Native Americans. This was due to the historical confusion caused by the label "Indian" and how it has been used in the United States. For example, I was frequently asked, "What are you?" by white Americans when they could not place my physical appearance. Despite answering that I am Indian American, follow-up responses included microaggressions like asking, "What kind of Indian are you?" My original reply "I'm Indian American" did not suffice and often met with disregard by further questioning that included "What tribe are you?" Unfortunately, attempting to use the Asian Indian American self-label created more confusion for some. At times this confusion was followed by insensitive comments and microaggressive racist slurs, such as "So, you're mixed? But you don't look Chinese," as they failed to understand that Asian Indian American did not mean that I was multiracial.

Being a Woman of Color in the United States throughout the 1970s, 1980s, and 1990s, who was not easily identified as part of one of the expected racial groups, I found myself wanting to learn what it was like for the people who shared the "Indian" label. Exploring the experiences of Native Americans across the nation helped me to understand my answer to the "what are you" question. Gaining clarity and having such discussions were critical to developing a South Asian American organization. Had Dr. White not emphasized expanding my knowledge base or modeled talking to diverse individuals in various geographical regions, I might have been limited in developing a culturally relevant and appropriate name for my organization.

Understanding the Inner Workings of Organizations

Dr. White freely shared his network by introducing students and colleagues to presidents, chairs, and leaders of organizations. In connecting individuals, he also provided financial support if and when needed to become a member of that organization and encouraged involvement beyond just membership. Mentees would often hear, "Become a member, get involved, get to know who the key players are and learn the inner workings of the organization." Dr. White's introductions to "Key Power Players" led to invitations to join convention planning committees, review conference proposals, judge poster sessions, and eventually rate journal articles. All these experiences were like windows into how organizational systems worked. I saw firsthand how agendas were pushed, how people advocated, why papers were accepted versus rejected, and how to effectively communicate in public and private forums. Dr. White often talked about how women and other people from marginalized communities needed to "learn the inside game" because they were excluded from dinners, happy hours, sporting events, and other informal and planned gatherings. Therefore, when I explained that I wanted to understand the inner workings of my profession and make a difference, I was advised to take the initiative to become part of professional organizations and systems. With that in mind, I chose to join the Society of Counseling Psychology (APA Division 17) and the Society for the Psychological Study of Culture, Ethnicity and Race (APA Division 45). Being a part of these groups gave me the opportunity to learn organizational cultures, understand how to approach tackling complex intuitional issues, build allies, contribute, and earn a positive reputation. My roles in these groups and on committees served as stepping stones to becoming an organizational leader (i.e., co-chair for the Division on Women for AAPA and later the vice president of AAPA) and contributed to my learning to create and maintain an organization. By understanding the inner workings of organizations through doing the work and using each opportunity as a stepping stone for creating change inside organizations for a more powerful outside impact, my vision was to become one of the "Key Power Players" (i.e., leaders in power who could create change, make decisions, and advocate for others) so that I could impact South Asian American mental health by expanding an existing organization and creating a new association.

Connecting at the Lowest Common Denominator

When around Dr. White, I carefully observed his interactions with people of all ages, stages, races, genders, classes, and professions. He had a way of connecting with most people in a genuine, caring, and empathic way. When I asked Dr. White about his ability to seamlessly connect with people, he said he paid attention to a person's "vibe," that natural chemistry and connection was easier with some than others in collaborating with them. In my observations of his skillful patience and attentiveness during social hours, or while "holding court" at hotel bars, I learned of his ability to converse and help individuals with challenging personalities (in other words, he connected with people that I personally found to be annoying). When I asked him about his ability to connect and see value in particular people, he confidently responded with "Look if you want to create change, get ahead in any organization and make a lasting impact, you've got to learn to connect with folks at the lowest common denominator." Meaning, whether you like someone or not, you have to find a way to build relationships, find common ground so you can learn *and* make a difference in this world. Dr. White would say, "Change can't happen if you're always fighting with folks, putting out bad energy and don't see eye to eye on things in an organization, you need to find the lowest common denominator and connect with people on that level." He was matter of fact about organizations being filled with unique personalities, and change would not happen if you could not connect with those you did not have anything in common with.

Dr. White's advice of connecting at the lowest common denominator was among the most critical pieces of advice to his mentees and probably the hardest mentoring advice to follow. Learning to connect at the lowest common denominator was critical to creating organizations and finding a way to collaborate with those who did not agree with your agenda and priorities socially, politically, or professionally. For example, I learned that creating new divisions (i.e., formally organized groups within the structure of a larger association) in psychological associations was met with both resistance and support among power players and members. Being able to connect with leaders despite differences was key to pushing forward on goals. Humility, respect, acknowledging differences, and even ignoring differences were skills needed to advocate and create new organizations when asking people for something that I needed. Fortunately, I learned to connect with people in multiple psychological organizations, both allies and doubters. I developed relationships based on minimal commonalities by intentionally sharing my agenda and striving for inclusivity in my invitations, with the goal of providing opportunity to join and collaborate. Finding ways to connect at the lowest common denominator was critical to developing the first-ever ethnic division within a psychological organization.

Creating Formalized Systems of Support and Organizations

With the lack of presence of South Asian American students, graduate students, professors, and clinicians, and Dr. White's early validation, I knew there was the need for a space and place for South Asian American counseling and psychology. During my early conventions, I perused the program book looking for symposiums. I tried to identify South Asian topic areas, searched for Indian sounding names, and attended their presentations. After their presentations, I would collect the presenters' names and let them know I would stay in touch. Over the course of a few years of this, I began to organize dinners bringing South Asian Americans together. Along with diverse allies, we would network, exchanging information and sharing knowledge prior to the start of AAPA and APA conventions to strategize about ways to make a positive impact outside of structured systems and organizations. I developed a network of like-minded individuals with whom I shared similar experiences, I found validation, and I felt hope and inspiration but most importantly did not have to explain who we were as South Asian American people. By the end of my time as an early career professional, I had come to understand how psychology organizations were built, how they operated, and how to make them work for you.

In 2001, myself and other Indian American co-founders created the South Asian Psychological Networking Association (SAPNA), which connected South Asian Americans, allies, and yes, doubters to gather for dinners prior to the national AAPA and APA conventions. As co-founders of SAPNA, Drs. Arpana Inman, Puni Kalra, Neera Puri, and I developed an email listserv and website that brought together over 400 individuals from the United States and abroad to share and exchange ideas. SAPNA was quite successful, and eventually, the interest and numbers of South Asian Americans entering the field of psychology were strong enough to create a formalized structure.

SAPNA was renamed as the Division of South Asian Americans (DoSAA) in the AAPA; just as ABPsi set the stage for an association for Asian Americans and other cultural professional organizations to follow, DoSAA has served as a model for other ethnic divisions within AAPA. The Division of Filipino Americans, the Division of Southeast Asians, and other divisions have seen been established, leading to greater expansion, inclusivity, and more seats at the table.

Rising Beyond the Organization

For Dr. White there was always a next step for continued growth, especially when it came to taking new professional advancement opportunities. He pushed mentees to keep evolving beyond their organizations. During our mentoring meetings, he would help me to evaluate my progress, asking me to state my goals beyond developing the organization that I set out to develop. He knew that personal and professional goals change, and he encouraged me to think toward onward, forward, and upward movement. Dr. White taught me not to stay complacent in any organization or structured environment. He explained that graduate programs, workplaces, and organizations could only take you so far (and sometimes even limited you).

Soon after I developed our organization and was settled in my job, he encouraged next-step thinking. In my case he planted the seeds for publishing based on the work from my organization, experiences, education, and clinical work. Once I successfully created a formalized system of support for South Asian Americans, the process started over again.

This time he helped me to land my first book contract, which led to the publication of *Asian American Psychology: Current Perspectives* (2009), co-edited with Alvin Alvarez, and to pay my learning and mentoring forward to mentees and riders on The Freedom Train. Creating an organization was almost a metaphor for Dr. White; it was about "creating something from nothing" in more ways than one, always looking at the big picture, even beyond organizations.

Practical Strategies and Best Practices

Realistically, most of us do not possess Dr. White's gifts, nor do we share his unique historical experiences as Black man. Additionally, it is impossible to identically emulate your mentor or mentors. However, over the decades, I have learned from Dr. White as a master mentor and found it possible to develop what I believe are practical strategies and best practices in my areas of competency. Therefore, in this section, I share my teachings by offering specific strategies, practices, and discussion questions that will help you operationalize your goals and optimize your success.

- **Networking** – This is an essential and must-do if you wish to develop an organization and expand in any way. The networking I am talking about goes beyond writing handwritten notes, making phone calls to check in, and follow-up letters or thank-you cards. What I am referring to is identifying who comprises your "Natural Networks" and "Strategic Networking." We all have existing networks; I encourage you to think about who naturally exists in your network without networking? Family, friends, neighbors, your social media network, your kids' friends' parents, etc. Most people think of networking as limited to co-workers, professional affiliations, and companies. However, the key is to be strategic in targeting groups you would not normally think of, in addition to reaching out, sharing, and seeking advice from those you least expect to receive feedback and guidance from.
- **Targeting Your Networking Communication** – When you do meet someone through networking personally or professionally, whether it is a cover letter, email, social media communication – my simple formula is to open with a positive greeting, remind the person of your conversation, and state the purpose of contacting them. The tone of your communication should reflect both care (interpersonal connection) and business in achieving your goals.
- **Connect with People at the Lowest Common Denominator** – If there are challenging individuals in your organization, bureaucratic system, or power structure, find a way to connect with them at the bare minimum commonality when your goal is advocacy or advancement.

Connecting with professionals is one aspect of achieving goals, but I advise that people extend their ability to connect with those at the lowest common denominator by not limiting such behavior to just professional relationships. I often emphasize the importance of this connecting in social relationships, with your extended family, neighborhood, and any other community to which you belong since connecting with people at the lowest common denominator is a critical skill at any life stage.

- **Natural Chemistry** – Some of the most fulfilling relationships are ones that you cannot "force." Seek fruitful relationships, whether in hiring, collaborating, or mentoring, that "do not feel like work" or "drain you" if you are in an organization or institution. Relationships with individuals where there is "Natural Chemistry" will often likely lead to authenticity, realness, transparency, reciprocity, and enjoyment when learning from one another.

- **Seek Differing Relationships** – Make a commitment to seek, reach, and mentor diverse individuals who are different from you. Share your resources. Work toward building powerful relationships across ages, races, and genders across the nation in multiple disciplines. Successful organizations benefit from individuals of varying mindsets, experiences, cultures, and locations. Flexibility is critical in devising plans and achieving your goals. The process of achieving goals and creating is most effective when multiple plans and pathways are devised to attain the end result. Openness to accepting opportunities not previously considered will allow you to make the best of a situation when plans do not work out in the way envisioned.

- **Credibility Markers** – Joining professional associations and reputable organizations, earning degrees, and seeking positions at reputable institutions are often credibility markers in professional spaces and careers. Additional credibility markers include publication or social media influence.

- **Collaboration** – I am a big believer in collaborative learning due to the exchange of ideas, information, and opportunity for feedback. If you wish to learn to publicly speak, then ask someone how to create speaking templates. If you wish to increase your organizations budget, then learn to write grant proposals from others. Effective collaboration also includes asking, giving, and receiving relevant information.

- **Considering Professional and Life Stages** – Depending on age, level of experience, and developmental life stage, I encourage young professionals in organizations or mentees to educate themselves on salary negotiation when relevant, maintaining positive relationships and not burning bridges in your industry, especially if you choose to remain in that profession. For mid-career professionals, I encourage this group of professionals to seek upward job promotions and consider flexibility in balancing family or personal life, new leadership roles, and other opportunities for financial and career advancement. My advice to seasoned leaders in professional organizations is to have discussions on how to consult, seek administrative roles, and plan for retirement when working with senior career professionals. Essentially, when working with employees or mentees, I do not use a one-size-fits-all approach. I am careful not to overwhelm with too much advice. My goal is to help identify what is most important to the individual and facilitate that which is most beneficial to them in their developmental stage.

- **Work with the Next Generation** – A huge component of success is connecting to students, colleagues, and younger people to stay current with new trends and innovation while imparting your wisdom to the next generation (not getting stuck in the zeitgeist of your times).

Discussion Questions

1   How do you feel about trying to create beneficial relationships across disciplines? How would you identify relevant disciplines or individuals worth connecting with?
2   How have you approached working with individuals you dislike? What are some ways you can connect with those individuals at the lowest common denominator?
3   How comfortable are you with marketing yourself? How might you use digital marketing and social media platforms to advance your career goals?

9 Embracing My Seat at the Table

Le Ondra Clark Harvey

Figure 9.1 Image of Le Ondra Clark Harvey with her son and Joseph L. White. Provided by and used with permission of Le Ondra Clark Harvey (2022).

DOI: 10.4324/9781003132899-12

Do for Others What I Do for You: The Freedom Train

A. Philip Randolph wrote, "Freedom is never given; it is won." This quote captures the essence of the struggle that one must endure on their road to true liberation. Black people know struggle. Though not fully liberated, we know the only key to liberation is joining together to overcome the structural, institutional, and individual forms of racism that keep our people enslaved. In the 1830s, the term "Underground Railroad" was coined when describing the patchwork of allies who worked together to help slaves find their way to the free North. Dr. White built off of that theme and created a "Freedom Train" to connect diverse students and professionals across the nation and promote excellence within and outside of the academy. I am a passenger on the Freedom Train. I have benefited from its shelter, learned from my fellow passengers, and participated in recruiting others to join us on the ride. In order to explain how I got to the train station, so to speak, I will begin by sharing my introduction to the field of psychology.

When I was a little girl, I remember my mother telling me and my sister that we could be anything we wanted to be. I believed her, but I could not figure out what that was. However, I definitely knew what I *did not* want to be. I did not want to be a mental health professional. My mother was a counselor, she had a private practice, and the clients she saw did not look like me or live in my neighborhood. So, I erroneously believed that mental health treatment was not for the young or the ethnically diverse.

Prior to starting college, I figured out that I wanted to be a news broadcaster. I majored in communications and journalism. One day, a friend challenged me and said, "Le Ondra, you talk about helping others and making a significant difference in the community, how can you do this if you're just a talking head on tv?" In the moment I responded sharply, but when I went home and took a long hard look in the mirror, I realized my friend was right. I enrolled in sociology and psychology classes the next quarter and fell in love with the study of individuals, their minds, their behavior, and how they are influenced by their families and communities. I realized that mental health disparities were striking among disenfranchised communities, and I became passionate about ameliorating this phenomenon. I quickly learned that I would need additional education in order to pursue this goal.

After changing my major to psychology, I applied to the McNair Scholars Program, a program in honor of the late Ronald Erwin McNair, a physicist and second Black to make a flight into space, ultimately dying during the Challenger space launch. The McNair Program provided diverse students the opportunity to receive extensive research training and opportunities to help prepare them for graduate school. The program taught me the fundamentals of research and provided me with stipends and scholarships to present my research within and outside of the United

States. With the funds from McNair, I was able to pay for the Graduate Record Examination (GRE) and the application fees for graduate programs I applied to. I imagine that Ronald McNair never fathomed that his untimely death would lead to a program that would significantly impact the educational trajectory of hundreds of thousands of young people. The McNair Program is an example of the Freedom Train movement. Unbeknownst to me, Dr. White had played a critical role in establishing the first Educational Opportunity Program (EOP) in California, which funds the McNair Scholars Program.

When it was time to apply to graduate programs, I remember my confidence as I prepared my applications. I had done everything the McNair Program had taught me to, and I had a robust research portfolio. However, that confidence was challenged during a conversation with one of my psychology professors. When I shared my list of schools with her, she balked,

> Well, those are very competitive schools ... many students desire to go to Research I universities, but find that it is too far from home; maybe you should reconsider and just stay in California where you can be a big fish in a smaller pond?

I was taken aback by her comments but decided to push forward with my applications as I remembered my mother's words "you can be anything you want to be."

A few days after submitting my applications to clinical psychology programs, I was perusing a website of one of the schools I applied to and stumbled upon their counseling psychology program. As I read about the tenets of the field and the focus on social justice and systems level change, I realized that this was the missing piece for me. While I had been well prepared to conduct clinical research, I had not figured out how this would allow me to serve my community in a way that fulfilled me. I assumed it would all come together during graduate school. However, the counseling psychology discipline seemed to be a beacon that was calling to me. I quickly contacted all the clinical psychology programs I applied to and asked them to set my application aside. I submitted several applications to counseling psychology programs and was accepted to every counseling psychology program that I applied to.

I chose to attend the counseling psychology program at the University of Wisconsin, Madison. Acclimating to graduate school was easy in terms of the academics, but attending school in the Midwest was a different cultural experience for me. Maybe, I thought, my professor was right. Maybe students of color do not do well in these places. However, because I was a McNair Scholar, I was linked to programs on campus that helped me stay connected to my community of racially and ethnically diverse graduate students and mentors. Despite the insidious racism

I felt off campus, I thrived within my department. Little did I realize that the Freedom Train that Dr. White had initiated was surrounding me the entire time.

During graduate school, I attained my license as a professional counselor and practiced at a community mental health center. I was passionate about providing services to individuals who represented disenfranchised communities. But, despite the fulfillment I gained from my clinical work and research, I felt restless. These moments of restlessness were the greatest when my advisor, Dr. Hardin Coleman, would broach the "scientist/practitioner" topic with me. He would say, "Le Ondra, there are hardly any Black professors in psychology – you should consider a career in academia. You can always practice on the side." My usual retort to my advisor was "I'm getting a Ph.D. because I want to do whatever I want to. I do not want to be bound by just two options for my future." However, similar to when I was a little girl, I still had not figured out what this was really going to look like.

I remember being selected to represent the counseling psychology student cohort as part of a faculty member hiring process. We interviewed several candidates, and I was most impressed by one candidate's professional experience. His name is Dr. Ezemenari Obasi. He had connections to California, having worked with Dr. White. I knew who Dr. White was because we had studied his work and his influence in my courses. Dr. Obasi was also an American Psychological Association Minority Fellowship Program (APA MFP) fellow. Ultimately, he did not choose to join the faculty, but we kept in touch over the years. He was the first individual to encourage me to apply to the APA MFP, and toward the end of my first year in my PhD program, I was selected as a fellow.

In many ways, the APA MFP was an advanced version of McNair. One of the programs MFP invited me to participate in was the Psychology Summer Institute – a summit for graduate students interested in health disparity research. During the summit, students were sent to Capitol Hill to lobby for the APA MFP. I had never done anything like this before. The visit I had with my representative's office was transformative for me. As well as talking about the APA MFP, we spoke extensively about my passion for working with disenfranchised populations. This experience inspired me to look for other opportunities to use my skills to impact the policy making process.

In 2007, everything started to come together in a way that made the Freedom Train most evident to me. I wrote earlier that I had heard about Dr. White from classes I took. Two professors, Drs. Angela Byars-Winston and Alberta M. Gloria, were instrumental in teaching me about Dr. White and several other racially and ethnically diverse pioneers in psychology. Dr. Gloria required that students research the ethnically specific psychology associations: (a) Association of Black Psychologists (ABPsi), (b) Society of Indian Psychology, (c) National Latinx

Psychological Association, and (d) the Asian American Psychology Association. This was the first time I learned that there was a psychology association for Black psychologists and trainees, and I joined immediately.

Dr. Gloria not only taught me about the Freedom Train, but she also allowed me to be a part of it. She invited me to mentor some of her Summer Fellows from California. These students, Cynthia Medina, Marlen Kanagui-Munoz, and Adisa Anderson, had all worked with Dr. White and were spending their summer doing research with Dr. Gloria at UW, Madison. I quickly discovered how extensive Dr. White's Freedom Train was. From his founding the EOP programs that would assist me with the skills to get accepted to a graduate school program, his work with scholars at UC Irvine such as Dr. Obasi who would encourage me to apply for the APA MFP, his work with Dr. Gloria who included me in the mentorship program for her UC Irvine summer interns, and his founding of ABPsi that would enhance my leadership and professional development, the Freedom Train had been surrounding and supporting me throughout my entire educational tenure.

A Chance Encounter

My graduate program placed high value on professional development. From Dr. Gloria introducing students to various professional psychology associations early in our tenure to all professors assisting students financially to attend conferences, this was an integral part of the department's culture. In fact, Dr. Gloria helped me fund my way to my first APA convention, allowing me and my other classmates to volunteer hours in a hospitality suite. Not only did we have a place to stay, but we were also able to network with dozens of psychologists – many of whom we only knew from their research articles we studied and chapters they wrote in our course textbooks.

I remember arriving at an APA meeting in Washington, D.C., one year. I was in the elevator of the Marriott Hotel, and a man was standing directly across from me, his head tilted down as he peered over the top of his glasses to read my name badge. "Hey, sister, you from Wisconsin?" he said. Hesitantly, I replied, "I'm from California, but I'm in graduate school at the University of Wisconsin, Madison." "Oh, a California girl!" He then stepped off the elevator and said a line I would hear him repeat hundreds of times, "Alright, keep doing what you are doing – keep the faith!" A few hours later, at the end of a busy convention day, I joined a group of students and professionals in the hotel lounge. The central figure of the busy table we gathered around was that stranger in the elevator, Dr. White. He laughed as I approached the table: "Hey, I want everyone to know that this sister would barely speak to me on the elevator." He reminded me of our first meeting whenever we saw one another over the years.

The gatherings at Dr. White's table became a safe place amid busy professional meetings where students and professionals could gather to laugh, learn, and receive advisement. This was all a part of Dr. White's "Freedom Train" strategy, to provide spaces where professionals could use their position and influence to empower proteges to succeed and then pay back the favor by doing the same for the next generation.

Dr. White would call and email me occasionally. If I won an award or got a promotion, Dr. White was one of the first people to find out and reach out. It amazed me that he was able to track the professional development of so many students and professionals. Then again, he had masterfully built a quilt of connected individuals that spanned the country. The Freedom Train had significant reach. After a few moments of congratulations, he would go into what I call "Freedom Train Mode," and an intentional line of questioning would ensue. It often sounded like, "Now, what's next? You just won this award, and you are going to get additional publicity. Here's who you need to talk to if your goal is to rise in this segment of the field." Then, he would shift to the "Pay it Forward" part of the conversation. It sounded like, "Okay, I met this student and I told her about you. I need you to call her and talk to her about ...". *He never rested. He kept on pushing.* His train only stopped to let people on.

Ironically, the last time I would sit at a table with Dr. White would be over a decade later in that same hotel lounge, shortly before he passed away. My friend and colleague, Dr. Bedford Palmer, set up the gathering. I was elated to introduce my one-year-old son to Dr. White. As I took a photo of the two of them sitting together in the lounge, memories flooded my brain. I thought about me sitting in that same spot with Dr. White over the years. I thought about the promise my child has and the hopes I have for him to be a part of a Freedom Train movement that will support him someday. This was the last time I sat at a table with Dr. White, and it was a beautiful final memory.

A Viral Video with a Reminder: You Cannot Seek Validation from Your Oppressor

One of the highlights of my time as a graduate student was interviewing Dr. White during the ABPsi's 40th Annual Convention on August 1, 2008. I was the chair of ABPsi's Student Circle and was asked by one of my mentors, Dr. Halford Fairchild, to be the interviewer for a video series he was creating. Dr. Fairchild reached out to dozens of ABPsi's elders and founding members in an effort to document their contributions to Black psychology. Though I had known Dr. White for a few years at this point, I was still a bit nervous to interview such a giant in the field but more so intrigued and impressed by his reflections. Little did I realize how popular this video interview would become. Dr. White's video has been viewed over 40,000 times online.

During the interview, Dr. White reflected on his upbringing. Not surprising, a train was an important feature of his story. He actually worked on a train as a waiter before relocating to California where he quickly discovered that there were no opportunities or union for Black waiters. He told me that this was the moment that he made a change in how he had envisioned his future. I felt a connection to Dr. White as he explained that; similar to my story, his path was influenced by a family member who was a mental health clinician. His aunt was a social worker and encouraged him to apply to college at San Francisco State University where he was introduced to the discipline of psychology.

Dr. White's tenacity was inspiring. He described how he broke barriers as one of the first Black students to complete the graduate program at Michigan State. He described the low expectations that faculty had of him: "They didn't think colored negro students had the capacity to do advanced graduate work, but I graduated in three years." These words resonated with me as I remembered the words that my professor had said to me years prior when she cautioned that going to graduate school in the Midwest would be too much of a cultural shift for me. Dr. White explained that upon graduation, he felt like he had "climbed the mountain." That is, until he returned to California and could not rent a house or office. He described his transformation from being "the nicest Negro to being a militant Negro. I had been operating with blinders." He recounted that Malcolm X's brother was one of ten Black graduate students enrolled at Michigan State at the time he was: "I thought I was somebody special; the talented tenth; Malcolm X and his brother were trying to tell me there was another reality out there."

The shift from the ivory towers of the academy to the harsh reality of being a Black man in California, who was not afforded the privileges of many of his counterparts, left an indelible mark on Dr. White. The structural and institutional racism he encountered fueled his desire to create opportunities for Black scholars to reach the communities they emerged from. Dr. White certainly accomplished this goal as he joined a group of young Black psychologists who would comprise the founding member class of the ABPsi.

Dr. White explained the four pillars of the Black psychology movement that fueled him and the other ABPsi co-founders:

1   Connectedness – Everyone needed the space and time to testify about their experience as a Black person in America;
2   Deconstruction – Black people were invisible in the discipline of psychology, so the science was incomplete; it merely reflected the beliefs of society;
3   Confrontation – Psychological science purported that Blacks were inferior, so Black psychologists need to make the scientific leader of the field, the APA, accountable for this erroneous characterization of Blacks; and,

4   Creativity – Black scholars cannot depend upon their counterparts
     to define them; they needed a strength-based view of their psyche
     that came from the people and was written in an understandable
     manner. They also needed their own organization committed to re-
     defining who Blacks are and how the people they serve can heal.

These tenets ring true today. Fifty-three years after the founding of
the ABPsi, the need to have the space to continue this work remains.
Dr. White and his fellow founders knew that ABPsi was a critical element
in helping Black scholars, such as myself, excel. Dr. White summed up his
understanding of his purpose in founding ABPsi and the Freedom Train
movement when he stated, "...because I was a teacher, I saw it as my
job to develop the next generation of Black psychologists ... everybody I
mentored was responsible for mentoring ... everyone from UC Irvine left
with an internalized definition of mentorship." He ended with an advisement: "Get on the Freedom Train and you'll get more choices."

Excellence Will Bring You Opportunity: Shaping Public Policy

Having a seat at the table does not guarantee that it is a comfortable one.
However, it is important to retain your seat in recognition of the many
individuals who have assisted in securing the seat for you. As a psychologist who works within the political arena, the influence I am able to exercise assists in opening doors and creating opportunities for those who
do not have the voice or privilege to advocate for themselves. The seat I
have been afforded has been influenced by so many, including Dr. White,
who was known for instilling in his mentees the belief that "Excellence
will bring you opportunity." With this in mind, I will share how the pursuit of excellence helped me to become a leader within a nontraditional
career field.

To this point, I have shared about my background and how Dr. White's
Freedom Train has been an ever-present force in my personal and professional development. More important is how the people and lessons I
learned helped to influence where my path has taken me.

Dr. White's Freedom Train exposed me to preeminent scholars. One
such individual was Dr. Vivian Ota Wang. Dr. White knew about my
passion for representing the voice of disenfranchised populations, and
he looked for opportunities to connect me to individuals who could provide mentorship to me. Not surprising, it was while we were sitting at a
table during an APA convention when Dr. White introduced me to an
individual who would significantly impact my career trajectory. Dr. Ota
Wang has worked for various U.S. presidential administrations as well as
for federal agencies including the National Institutes of Health. She was
the person I would reach out to when contemplating a career change and
who ultimately influenced my entrance to the public policy arena.

I remember feeling perplexed after completing my postdoctoral fellowship at UCLA Mattel Children's Hospital. I was offered a full-time position to continue working at UCLA, but I did not feel content with accepting the offer. I had been working at the hospital providing services to families that had adopted children from the foster care system. It did not take long to notice that I was one of the only clinicians who enjoyed driving to impoverished neighborhoods to provide clinical services. While the thought of working full-time at a premiere research and clinical institution seemed like the perfect attainment of my goals, I knew that I would not be fulfilled. It was this feeling that fueled my desire to begin looking for opportunities for psychologists to engage with public policy.

I discovered a program that placed PhD scientists at the California State Capitol for one-year fellowships. Now, when I first found this program, I almost passed on the opportunity to apply. When I looked at the alumni, all were natural scientists and engineers. A voice crept into my head, "This isn't for you ... they don't want behavioral scientists in this program." However, as I had done dozens of times before, I sent the website link to Dr. Ota Wang. She immediately wrote back that this opportunity was "perfect" for me and that I should apply, and she was right. I was the first behavioral health scientist accepted to the California Council on Science and Technology Fellowship program in 2012.

What I thought would be a one-year fellowship quickly turned into six years of service at the California State Legislature that would build the foundation for a career in the public policy arena. My unique training as a psychologist, my passion for advocating for disenfranchised populations and my work ethic combined made me a standout and gave me the opportunity to excel within the system. By the time I had completed six years at the Capitol, I had established a portfolio of excellent work products and demonstration of leadership in both the Senate and Assembly. I was the youngest, first female, and first Black Chief Policy Consultant of the Business, Professions and Economic Development Committee at the State Assembly. I do not share my success to brag but to make a point. It was the academic preparation, support of mentors, combined with grit and hard work that enabled me to excel. The lessons I learned from Dr. White about mentorship, pursuit of excellence, and paying it forward helped me become a leader within an arena I did not initially envision myself working within.

Everything Comes Full Circle: Keep the Faith

At this point in my career, I am beginning to see how all the lessons I learned from Dr. White and colleagues whom I have met on the Freedom Train have coalesced in a way that has allowed me to find purpose in my career. My tenure at the Capitol led me to an opportunity to be an advocate and leader for community mental health and substance use clinics in California. I am the chief executive officer of the California Council of Community Behavioral Health Agencies, which is an organization that represents the interests of behavioral health community-based organizations across the state. This position is a marriage of my passions for advocating for disenfranchised populations while leveraging the skills I developed while working at the State Legislature. It affords me the opportunity to be the voice for so many who are working in the trenches at community-based organizations like I used to. I also have the privilege of telling the stories of the clients who depend on vital behavioral health services to those who sit in positions of power. I know that the journey is not over, and I look forward to what will happen next in my career. In the meantime, I am committed to advancing the Freedom Train.

Practical Strategies for Being an Effective Advocate and Mentor

I have shared about my journey to public policy and how Dr. White has influenced my path. This journey would be meaningless if I did not share the information that has been critical in shaping me into an effective advocate and mentor on the Freedom Train. Below, I will share a few tips that serve as guiding principles for my professional and personal life.

1   Write a mission statement – Someone once challenged me to articulate my mission statement for my career. A mission statement is a reflection of one's values and passions. I encourage this activity as it can help one think about the purpose and meaning behind their professional pursuits.
2   Passion is a critical element – Once you have determined what your mission statement is, let your passion guide your decisions. If you do not believe fully in something, or you are not energized by it, it will eventually fail, or you will become complacent and ineffective.
3   Seek out mentorship and support – Who you choose as a mentor is a critical decision. First, they must want to mentor you, must be invested in your personal mission, and willing to keep you accountable to it. It is important to discriminate who you share your dreams with – not everyone needs to know them – some things should be kept close to your heart until they mature and only shared with those who believe in your dreams and are willing to push you further than you thought you could go. And, always have someone in your mentorship circle who is older and wiser and younger and smarter.
4   Your career is a team sport – No one arrives where they are at by themselves. Community is critical in helping you advance in your career. Once you have gained some success, remember to develop protégés and cultivate your replacement. Pay it forward – success should be shared.

5 Be careful how you use your power – Power comes in many forms, and it is not eternal. As such, understand your power, the political ramifications of it, and use it wisely. Your influence can build a person up or tear them down completely, and you never know when you might need that person's help.

6 Handle mistakes gracefully – Remember that mistakes are a part of life; it is how you recover that says the most about you.

7 Engage in self-care – Self-care is a critical aspect of being successful, and it is oftentimes the most difficult thing for professionals to integrate into their lives. I was listening to a motivational speaker during a board retreat years ago. She created a "Self-care bill of rights." I still have a note card on my desk with the bill of rights typed on it, and it reads:

- *You have the right to say no.*
- *You have the right to prioritize your mental, physical, emotional, and spiritual well-being.*
- *You have the right to make decisions about your time without guilt.*
- *You have the right to adequate sleep.*
- *You have the right to define success for yourself.*
- *You have the right to serve your community in a way that makes you come alive.*

Discussion Questions

1 I have written about how the Freedom Train was a present force in my life represented by programs Dr. White founded or influenced and people whom Dr. White mentored. As you reflect on your own journey, how do you see elements of the Freedom Train present in your life?

2 In my personal story as well as Dr. White's, there were individuals in our families whose personal career choice influenced our respective decisions to pursue an academic degree in a behavioral health discipline. How have individuals in your family influenced your beliefs about pursuing higher education?

3 Dr. White and the founding members of the ABPsi established four pillars of the Black psychology movement: (a) connectedness, (b) deconstruction, (c) confrontation, and (d) creativity. As you reflect on these pillars, which ones do you believe are still relevant today? How can you work to impact the underlying problems that ail the Black community? How can you work to dismantle the structural and institutional racism and barriers that impact the way the discipline of psychology is taught and the way it is enacted in clinical practice?

Section IV

Future Recommendations – "Don't Look for Validation in the Faces of Your Oppressor"

10 Navigating Toxic Privilege

Keep Your Fate in Your Own Hands

Bedford Palmer II and Michael E. Connor

Figure 10.1 Image of Michael Connor, Bedford Palmer II, Jenee Palmer, Joseph L. White, Coties Palmer (background), and Thomas Parham (seated) at Palmer Wedding. Provided by and used with permission of Bedford Palmer II (2022).

One of the most poignant messages that Dr. White shared with me was first delivered while I sat in the front row of my Black Baccalaureate Ceremony a couple of days prior to graduating with my bachelor's degree from the University of California, Irvine (UCI). At the time, I was the chair of our Afrikan Student Union (ASU), and I had been heavily involved in the planning and execution of the event. I had not really gotten

DOI: 10.4324/9781003132899-14

to know Dr. White, though I had seen him speak and share space at events.

Being the chair of the ASU, I styled myself one of the most militant Brothas on campus. I had protested to reestablish affirmative action in the state of California, called out racism in our campus newspaper, prevented a fraternity from holding a slave auction on campus, and pushed to literally have a seat at the table when administrators used ASU money to bring an internationally recognized speaker to campus but did not credit or involve our leadership in the decision. Like many young activists, I thought I had a handle on whiteness and how to deal with it. Then I saw Dr. White in action.

I will never forget the day of the Black Baccalaureate. We were in a medium-sized lecture hall at UCI in the Social Sciences complex. The room was filled with Black people, which was uncommon at my predominately Asian and white institution, where Black students accounted for less than 1% of the population. At the front of the room, soon-to-be Black graduates sat in the center rows of the audience, while to our left, university leaders and other VIPs sat in what I hope was more than performative support of our event and my peers.

We sat in anticipation, waiting to hear from our keynotes and to see the results of our graduate video of thank-you messages to our family and friends. I do not know what I expected when Dr. White began to speak. I probably thought he would talk about our potential and our struggle in the way I had seen him do during more public speaking engagements. And that is what he did, for the most part, as he provided the graduates with his "Keys to Being a Successful Black Person in the US." He spoke about creativity and resilience, as well as keeping a sense of humor and being open to support. His words were sage, and his delivery was just as engaging as any Southern Baptist preacher or skilled lecturer.

As he wrapped up his address, Dr. White had framed his talk by telling us that he would give us five keys to success, but that if we were a good audience, he would also share one more secret key. Accordingly, we were all waiting for the secret key as he completed his keynote address. The entire audience was hanging on his words when, in front of a mixed crowd, including the mostly white leadership of the university, he looked over his glasses at the Black graduating class of 2001 and told us to "Never put our fates in the hands of white folks."

This was a profound moment for me as a young Black man who styled himself as an activist. I remember hearing him make this proclamation and immediately sitting lower in my seat. I felt my peers doing the same, but then something amazing happened. In fact, the amazing thing was that nothing happened at all. There were no loud exclamations or agitated shuffling. The university leadership did not storm the stage. The University of California Police Department (UCPD) did not burst into the room and pull Dr. White from the podium. Instead, he continued his talk, and I sat a bit straighter as I listened to his rationale for healthy skepticism regarding cross-racial power relationships.

Dr. White was a master orator and storyteller. Better said, he was a master teacher in every sense of the word. In this room filled with students, their families, university faculty, staff, and administrators, Dr. White elicited head nods and murmurs of affirmation while telling Black students not to trust white people. He did this by grounding himself in reasonableness. His argument was not passionate, nor was it meant to burn the skin of the white folks in attendance. Instead, it was a clear citation of the relationship between a history of racism and oppression, the reality that society pressures everyone to conform to these power relationships, and the fact that if people relax for even a minute, they will invariably regress to the social norm. Dr. White explained to my graduating class that there was a danger in forgetting this relationship between power and whiteness. His message was not to distrust the personal character of individual white people but instead to know and understand that having good personal character does not make white people immune to centuries of social engineering. And thus, as long as racism is the societal norm, to protect oneself and one's success, a Black person must always remain skeptical of whiteness.

Navigating White Privilege in the Real

After graduating from UCI with a major in anthropology and a minor in African American studies, I realized that based on my activism, experiences as a peer counselor for first-generation college students, and my fascination with culture, I wanted to pursue a career in psychology. As one might expect, coming to this conclusion post-graduation might pose challenges in terms of the next steps. Luckily for me, my older sister was a mentee to Drs. White and Thomas Parham. Based on her advice, I sought out meetings with both. As Dr. Parham was a mentee of Dr. White, I experienced being conducted to my seat on the Freedom Train (i.e., Dr. White's mentorship network) by both the engineer and one of his closest conductors.

During these meetings, I chose to aim for a master's degree before applying to doctoral programs. I remember sitting across from Dr. White as he asked me if I wanted to try to apply directly to doctoral programs. I knew that I had not done all the coursework in psychology that I would need to be prepared for a doctoral program. I also understood that he was giving me the space to come to this conclusion on my own instead of him imposing limitations that I might feel diminished by (did I mention that Dr. White was a highly skilled psychologist and a master teacher).

In the end, I eventually found myself in a master's program in psychology at California State University, Long Beach (CSULB). There I worked to build my understanding of the general field of psychology, emphasizing developing skills as a researcher. And it was there that I also began to apply Dr. White's philosophy concerning maintaining a healthy skepticism in terms of white people within white systems of power.

I remember several incidents of racist microaggressions and macro-aggressions while working through this graduate education experience. From forming a bond with a group of students who held a diverse array of marginalized identities to force the discussion of multicultural issues in our courses, to having a white woman classmate try to appropriate my work, and having a professor tell me that maybe psychology was the wrong discipline for me instead of helping me to understand the statistical concept that I had brought questions about during office hours. Through all of this, I found that it was helpful to remember that I needed to protect myself and my goals. Looking back, I believe one of the benefits of Dr. White's message of skepticism was that I could insert doubt into any messages from the environment that I somehow did not belong in graduate school. This was a helpful buffer against the effects of feeling like an imposter (i.e., internalizing the belief that I did not deserve my place in my graduate program and the fear that I would be eventually found to be an imposter by my professors and my peers) (Ewing, Richardson, James-Myers, & Russell, 1996). That said, one of the most challenging obstacles to completing my master's degree came from a critical lack of skepticism.

As I moved through my master's program, I was presented with some choices that would define my trajectory as a scholar. One of the first was finding a faculty advisor, which was not a difficult decision. Only one faculty member shared my interests in serving Black communities and was part of Dr. White's Freedom Train. This faculty member was Dr. Michael Connor, a full professor who happened to be a Black man and literally Dr. White's first mentee. Dr. Connor helped to shepherd me through the difficult path of trying to develop as a social justice oriented Black psychologist within an academic department that did not share my interests.

This incongruency in scholarly interests between myself and the majority of the faculty became a barrier when it came time for me to write my master's thesis. It was difficult to find a thesis chair who could support me through this culminating work. Though my first choice for thesis chair was Dr. Connor, I was told that he could not act as my chair due to his changing status to part-time retirement. Dr. Connor's change of status and the department's systemic inflexibility forced me to look to professors whose work was not related to my focus on cultural factors and African-centered worldview.

To identify a professor who might be interested in working with me and understanding that this choice would not be based on scholarly similarity, I approached professors with whom I had positive past experiences. There was one white professor who I thought I had a reasonably good relationship with and who had connected with me based on our shared interest in science fiction. In this assumption of connection, I failed to engage in a healthy level of skepticism. I did not read between the lines when Dr. Connor was surprised by my decision and when he told me as much. In the present, as a faculty member myself, I have a much clearer understanding of how one must code their language to try to alert a student of a potential mistake concerning working with an unfriendly colleague. However, at the time, I believe I was so desperate to have an option that I ignored his warning and pressed forward even as the white professor provided no guidance related to the content of my project.

In my mind, the white professor was helping me by challenging my construct and pushing me to think harder about culture. I did not, at the time, understand that if he were actually supportive, he would have gone beyond challenging my conceptualization of culture and would have instead provided me direction on how to deepen my understanding of the construct and suggested alternatives. I also did not find it odd that he would defer to Dr. Connor, as one of my committee members, to act as my chair in terms of scholarly mentorship. And I did not understand that as my chair neglected to provide this scaffolding, he set me up for failure at my proposal meeting.

Yet, with Dr. Connor's help, I was able to prepare a thesis proposal that my thesis committee easily approved. Though critical, during that meeting, my committee members expressed excitement about my work. And based on Dr. Connor's coaching, I was able to anticipate and field any questions that came, which also meant that I did not have to rely on my chair for support and protection.

After my proposal was approved, the next step was to submit it for institutional approval for human subjects research. Though approval was not guaranteed, with the help of one's chair, it was mostly a formal learning opportunity as one moves to the long task of (pre-advent of the online survey) data collection. However, as I completed the institutional review application, I found myself in a crisis created by my chair.

It is important to note that this crisis was a deeply illustrative example of how one might engage in institutionalized violence against a student without having to act overtly racist. To help understand the violence of my chair's behavior, it is essential to explain that this action took place after a year of working on a thesis proposal. Each proposal draft was approved by my chair and eventually by my thesis committee. It is also important to understand that before beginning this yearlong proposal process, I spoke candidly with my soon-to-be thesis chair about the focus of my work, asking him directly if he would be able to support my research inquiry into cultural factors. He answered in the affirmative and agreed to work with me.

With this in mind, one might imagine the level of panic that I experienced when this white professor, who I had trusted with my scholarly development, explained to me that though he and my thesis committee had approved my proposal, he was uncomfortable signing my institutional review paperwork. He explained that he was unfamiliar with the cultural constructs that I would be measuring and suggested that I have Dr. Connor sign the application for me. However, as he knew, this was not possible as the application (i.e., the university) required the signature of the thesis chair. And hence, through inaction, my thesis chair attempted to force me to restart my master's thesis from scratch after a successful proposal.

My master's degree program was designed to take three years to complete. Students were expected to develop and defend their thesis proposal during their second year and then complete the associated empirical study and full write-up to defend as the culmination of their work in their third year before graduation. My thesis chair attempted to force me to restart my project and delay my graduation by at least a year but more likely cause me to wash out of the master's program due to frustration. Also, keep in mind that I was not, by any means, a struggling student. I was on track to not only be accepted by a doctoral program but also be accepted by ten of the top programs in the United States and be offered full funding in all but a few programs (those offering almost full funding). However, at the moment that my chair passive-aggressively refused to sign my Institutional Review Board (IRB) paperwork to sabotage my approved project, I had no idea what my future academic aspirations would be.

After a good amount of confusion and panic, I went to speak to Dr. Connor. I asked him for advice on how to deal with this situation and whether there was anything he could do to clarify these constructs to my thesis chair. He let me know that my chair's behavior did not surprise him, though the timing puzzled him. He explained that the time to try to stop my thesis project was probably before I successfully defended my proposal. He also told me that he would be happy to replace my thesis chair but was constrained by the department's new part-time retirement policy. He then advised me to talk to the department chair to see what could be done.

Though Dr. Connor expressed support, I was somewhat disappointed that he did not just ride to my rescue. I was oblivious to many of the constraints placed on Black faculty by expectations of collegiality, which I now understand to be another white supremacist control that tends to be unevenly enforced, leaving white faculty the option to pick and choose when and how or whether to engage with collegiality. When I met with the department chair, many things fell into place from my meeting with Dr. Connor.

After several attempts to meet with the department chair, I was finally able to pin him down with the help of an administrative staff member with whom I had developed a high level of rapport over the years (i.e., we were the same kind of book/movie nerd). I remember catching him on his office phone line and explaining the situation to him. I expected that he would immediately understand the issue and work out some compromise to facilitate the signing of my paperwork. But instead, he offered to let me restart my proposal.

At that point, many things happened at once. First, I realized that the department was in opposition to my completing my master's degree. Second, it became clear that the problem was not administrative but instead that it was the same tacit disregard for my well-being that I recognized from encounters with racist teachers and authority figures in the past. It is a particular kind of obtuseness that may have best been portrayed in the movie *The Shawshank Redemption* when Andy Dufresne asked the warden to help him prove his innocence, but the warden would not lift a finger. If you have ever experienced it, you can hear the humanity leave someone's voice as the empathy drains from their face. I heard this as this man casually attempted to unmake me. The third thing that happened was understanding that I was in a fight against racism. I remembered that Dr. White had shown me how not to be afraid. I remembered that the best way to move forward would be to systematically employ the truth. And finally, the last thing that happened was that I replayed my conversation with Dr. Connor in my head and realized that I had all the truths that I needed.

As I let my voice drain of the panic and plaintive anxiety that I had just been feeling, I felt more grounded and self-assured. Finally, understanding that neither the department chair nor my thesis chair had my best interest in mind or that they could be trusted to be fair, I decided that instead of seeking their approval, I would secure their compliance. And though I understood that I held much less power than either of them, there was a truth that I could leverage.

I remembered how Dr. Connor expressed surprise at the timing of my chair's attack. Then, hearing the department chair state that I "would just need to find another topic," I remembered that when I signed the paperwork acknowledging that my proposal was accepted by my committee, I was admonished to remember that my accepted defense constituted a contract between myself and the university (not the graduate department). The agreement was that I would complete my proposed thesis, or basically, I would be in jeopardy of not being allowed to earn my degree.

During my defense, I understood this as a way to ensure that students were accountable and did not try to change their topic after approval. However, when I responded to my department chair, I realized that the contract was binding both ways. The department could not bar me from completing my approved master's thesis based on a professor not wanting to help me anymore. With this in mind, I responded to the department chair's proposal with confusion. I explained that I did not understand his response as it was not aligned with the contract that I signed with the university. I explained that I knew that he and the psychology department would not want to breach a contract, so I wondered what "we" should do.

At that moment, I made it clear to him that I was informed about my rights, and by using legal terms like "breach of contract," I communicated that I planned to assert those rights in court, if necessary. I did this without threatening him outright, as I understood that a direct power struggle might end in him digging in his heels to defend his position and delaying or even successfully overcoming my argument. Instead, in framing it as a dilemma for us both to fix, I allowed him to take the path of least resistance (Johnson, 2001). After a short silence, the department chair agreed that this was, in fact, a dilemma. He explained that it might make more sense to replace my thesis chair, and I explained another truth that it would be hard to do, as there were few faculty in our department who had expertise in the area that I was focused. I then presented him with my last piece of truth, which was that it was a shame that Dr. Connor was not allowed to chair papers due to his part-time retirement, as he had originally expressed willingness and he was already on my committee. At that, the department chair perked up and informed me that there might be some flexibility in part-time retirement rules and that he would look into some things.

A few hours after ending the conversation, I received a call from Dr. Connor explaining that the department chair had asked him to take over as my thesis chair. Dr. White used to say that "you gotta learn to make something from nothing." In this case, though I found myself in a situation where support was being withheld, Dr. Connor facilitated a bubble of safety where I could move forward with my work without relying on the goodwill of people who had demonstrated the lack thereof.

Soon after commencing my thesis project, I spoke with Dr. Connor about the process. He explained that though he understood what was likely to happen between me and my former thesis chair, he could not truly predict the outcome. As he spoke, I realized that I only understood a small part of the power dynamics of my department. As with many graduate students, I believed that my faculty generally had things figured out. I felt that there was nothing to worry about if they were not openly disdainful toward me. Dr. Connor reminded me that the faculty were all just regular people, interacting in regular people ways, influenced by the same societal norms as everyone else.

Put plainly, I needed to remember that the same racism that was everywhere outside of academia was also everywhere inside of academia. Based on my experiences as a student from kindergarten to graduate school, I am at a loss for how I let myself forget. Dr. Connor let me know that he had hoped that everything would work out but that he made sure to provide me with information that I would be able to use to defend myself. He also explained that he was proud of how I was able to handle the situation, as the exception that the department made for him to chair my thesis could then be used to justify him chairing my classmate's thesis. This meant that she would not have to jump through the same hoops, though we knew she would still get hit with her own.

In conversations with Dr. White, when making an encouraging point, he would commonly employ a set of statements of reality. After each statement, he would ask, "am I right or am I wrong?" For example, when I doubted my ability to succeed as a student, he would remind me that I had succeeded as an undergrad that I was accepted to many graduate programs and that I had done well in my classes so far, following each statement with "am I right or am I wrong?" In doing this, he forced me to acknowledge the reality of my lived experience. In this same way, to navigate white privilege, one must live within the fact that white supremacy exists. It is regularly employed both intentionally and through semiconscious adherence to systemic racism.

To combat an intentionally racist attack from my thesis chair, I had to first acknowledge that it was, in fact, an attack and then realistically engage with the systemic racism that I would find in any business, organization, or academic department developed within the Western society. In this case, whether my department chair was intentionally supporting racism or he was only following the path of least resistance, it was in my interest to work within the reality of the situation and to make it clear that the path of least resistance led to me completing the thesis that the university agreed to.

Practical Strategies

Over the course of this chapter, I have attempted to convey the need for people from marginalized communities to be intentional about protecting their interests within a context of privilege and oppression. I spoke from my context as a Black man. However, the lessons that I tried to convey are not limited to a Black/white racial context. As Black people (and other People of Color) must never forget the danger of assuming safety with whiteness, so must women be vigilant of men, religious minorities be vigilant of Christians, poor people be vigilant of the rich, differently abled people be vigilant of able-bodied, and members of LGBTQIA+ communities be vigilant of the cisgender and heterosexual people. Below are some practical strategies for people from marginalized groups to employ, subject to contextual modification, when faced with systemic oppression.

- **Focus on facts, not fantasy or ego.** To address systemic oppression, we must be open to the truth, whatever it is. We must understand both our strengths and vulnerabilities to choose the correct strategy. Sometimes we must decide whether or not we are in the best position to push back. It can be better to wait while you shore up any weakness to ensure that your resistance will be more likely to succeed.
- **Accessing the environment.** Similar to being honest about your own circumstance, it is important to pay attention to the environment

that you are working within. We must be aware of the ground under our feet and the people around us. There are some spaces where your resistance is likely to meet with catastrophic failure if you approach from the wrong angle. Ask yourself, "what support do I have," "how tolerant are these people to feedback/pushback," "what motivates this organization/person," and "how much abuse can they get away with?"

- **Being Goal/Results Oriented.** I regularly see people focus on emotional satisfaction in their resistance, only to fail to make the gain that they were advocating for. It is vital that we identify our goal in every interaction with oppressive systems. You will often be faced with the choice between feeling good and making progress. Stated another way, we must often choose whether we want to win strategically or win morally. In my experience, the people who I serve would rather me win them the strategic gain and are less worried about whether I get an ego boost out of it.

- **Oppression demands silence – don't accept it.** In teaching classes on social justice advocacy, I like to describe white supremacy as an ever-present specter-like monster in the mirror that wants us to worry will manifest if we name it three times. I explain that instead, we must understand it to be the enormous ever-present monster that already has us in its grips, but that weakens every time we call its true name. We are taught throughout our lives that mentioning oppression is taboo, and it is. This is because oppressive forces deem it to be. Your first act of resistance must be acknowledging the reality of the oppressions that are leveled against you. To truly be free, you must recognize the oppressions that you level against others.

- **Strategic interventions (process statements).** Psychologists use process statements to call out the reality they are observing in a space. It is a way to help facilitate awareness of the dynamics at play and the effects on the people who are present. Process statements can be an observation or a question. For example, when interacting with oppressive systems, sometimes using a process statement to remind the people around you of the power dynamics in the room or the commitments to equity and inclusion that have been made can help undermine those power dynamics or inspire reconnection with those commitments. An important technical note is that the focus of the process statement is your experience of the space, not an attack on people within the space. This distinction is not about protecting oppressors; it is about reducing defensive responses and *being goal and results.*

- **Defining and maintaining boundaries – assertiveness.** It is essential to determine the limits of both what you will engage in and what you will endure. Oppressive systems seek to erode and redefine the boundaries of people who are from marginalized groups to the point of redefining our realities. To stave this off, we must define and bolster our own boundaries and live in reality as we assess it. A key to effectively defining and maintaining boundaries is the use of need-based or assertive communication. There are whole books on this, so take some time to google the concept. In short, assertive communication clearly defines one's needs and diminishes the likelihood of a defensive response (i.e., becoming combative or digging one's heals in) (Pipas & Jaradat, 2010). When interacting with oppressive systems, this looks like communicating your personal boundaries (e.g., I am uncomfortable with nonconsensual touching), work boundaries (e.g., this diversity project is outside of my scope of work; therefore, I would require separate compensation for this extra labor), intolerance of abuse (e.g., it is difficult to speak when others speak over me, or I find it discomforting when my ideas are restated as they tend to be reattributed and credited to the person who paraphrased me), or refusal to take part in oppressive behavior (i.e., I am uncomfortable with the way that Black students are being discussed in this meeting).

- **Understanding white tears and anger.** In relation to challenging oppression, negative reactions from those in power, regardless of how they are expressed, are generally dangerous to people from marginalized groups (Accapadi, 2007). That said, we must understand that the expression of tears and the expression of anger are both meant to silence the marginalized. Put simply, it is not your job to manage their behavior, nor is it your job to make anyone feel less bad about behaving in oppressive ways. Be mindful of the feeling to comfort or even attend to these behaviors, and instead consider using a process statement like "I can see that you are in pain, and my first instinct is to take care of you; however, I will trust you to take care of yourself, and we can continue when you are ready." Or if the negative behavior is sabotaging a meeting, "I care about your well-being, and I want you to take the time you need, but we are going to continue the discussion."
- **Accepting and embracing who you are (i.e., having a consistent curriculum vitae [CV] or resume).** After experiencing being attacked for my interest in social justice and cultural factors during my master's degree program, I decided that I did not want to work within a program that did not want to work with my whole self. With this in mind, I modified my academic resume (i.e., CV) to clarify that I was focused on work that involved Black people, cultural factors, and social justice. Since then, I have maintained this transparency in every professional setting. This has afforded me a level of freedom that would be denied if I had tried to hide who I was, as those who choose to work with me expect that I will be me and focus on the things that I focus on.

That said, this can be a risky strategy. First, you must be clear about who you are. I have been able to successfully use this strategy because I have also been consistent both in my areas of interest and my ability to produce excellence through my work. As you think about presenting yourself, make sure you know both what you are good at and what you want to involve yourself with. Also, be honest about the spaces that you seek to enter. I avoid some spaces as I know they would be unwelcoming, and even if I were successful there, it would be at the cost of my well-being.

- **Walking the walk – use your understanding of your own privilege.** Oppressive systems thrive on pitting one marginalized group against another. Whether it is across racial and ethnic groups or based on other intersectional identities (i.e., the various mixes of power-oriented identities that each of us hold) (Crenshaw, 1989), resistance to oppression is often met with a zero-sum response. Without delving into the deep complexity of intersectional realities, the simplest way to avoid this type of conflict is to be inclusive in your resistance. By this, I mean that we must move beyond simple self-defense in terms of resisting oppression. As a practical tactic, we must embrace a holistic social justice whereby we not only call out the oppression that we experience but also acknowledge and address the oppression in which we participate. Committing to this type of congruent behavior reduces the chance of being pit against another marginalized group and provides you with insight into how people with privilege will likely respond to your resistance. Stated plainly, they will react the way that you react when your privilege is challenged.

Discussion Questions

1   What are your reactions to the idea that you should never put your fate in the hands of those in privilege? How do you feel in your body? What does this challenge in you?

2   What strategies do you use to keep yourself grounded when dealing with oppressive systems? What kind of self-care do you engage in? When things do not seem to make sense, who do you talk to (or wish you could talk to)?

3   What are some boundaries you immediately set in your workplace, at school, at home, or in other social settings? How confident do you feel that you can communicate those boundaries effectively, and what strategies might you employ?

4   How have you dealt with conflict in the past? When you are in a conflict, what types of outcomes make you feel most successful in your interaction?

5   Which of your identities hold societal privilege? What type of work have you done to address the ways that you participate in the oppression of others? Are you doing as much work as you would expect of people who have engaged in oppressive behaviors toward you?

References

Accapadi, M. M. (2007). When White Women Cry: How White Women's Tears Oppress Women of Color. *College Student Affairs Journal, 26*(2), 208–215.

Crenshaw, K. (1989). Demarginalizing the intersection of race and sex: A black feminist critique of antidiscrimination doctrine, feminist theory and antiracist politics. *University of Chicago Legal Forum, 1989* (1), 139–167.

Ewing, K. M., Richardson, T. Q., James-Myers, L., & Russell, R. K. (1996). The relationship between racial identity attitudes, worldview, and African American graduate students' experience of the imposter phenomenon. *Journal of Black Psychology, 22*(1), 53–66.

Johnson, A. (2001). *Power, Privilege & Difference.* Mountain View, CA: Mayfield Publishing Co.

Pipas, M. D., & Jaradat, M. (2010). Assertive communication skills. *Annales Universitatis Apulensis: Series Oeconomica, 12*(2), 649.

11 Permission to Succeed

Jerell B. Hill

> But as for you, continue in the things that you have learned and of which you are convinced *holding tightly to the truths*, knowing from whom you learned them.
>
> (2 Timothy 3:14)

Right Place, Right Time

I often heard elders say that time and chance happen to everyone. Indeed, just that happened to me. Meeting Dr. Joseph L. White resulted from being in the right place at the right time. I received an invitation from Dr. Bedford Palmer II to attend the Association of Black Psychologists (ABPsi) conference in Los Angeles that year. This turned out to be a life-changing event. Meeting Dr. White was like a space where the environment was lively. It's like when someone is giving you pearls of wisdom but on an informal level where you can just talk in a free-flowing manner. This allowed me to unravel concepts that have served me well over time.

When I spoke to Dr. White, it was like talking to a successful relative or a spiritual godfather. I was inspired by his iconic status and the amount of work that it took for him to achieve such a high level of esteem, so I paid close attention to the lessons that he offered. So, as I sat in the lobby of the Los Angeles Marriott, having a good time while connecting with other professionals, I was humbled by the way that he included me in his circle and shared his knowledge so freely.

I listened while Dr. White told incredible stories of perseverance. I fondly remember him describing how after he graduated from his doctoral program that he ran home to look in the mirror. He explained that he had never seen a Black psychologist before. It moved me to think about what he must have gone through in order to successfully complete his doctorate as one of the first Black men to push his way into that field. However, he did not spend very much time speaking about his struggles, beyond how he made sure that everyone in his program knew that he was working harder than them. Instead, he focused on how he worked to provide a road for others to succeed. He would share about the "Freedom Train," his ever-growing informal organization of mentees, and I began

DOI: 10.4324/9781003132899-15

to see that there is a certain power that develops from embracing community and collaboration over individualism and competition.

Though this was not a totally new idea for me, I was interested to hear his perspective and how I could genuinely achieve freedom thought working with others. As with any new rider on the Freedom Train, I learned that I must look after people coming up after me once I came aboard. Dr. White explained that we were "future leaders that must transform systems that utilize conceptual pitfalls that prevent people from moving towards empowerment." I took from this that he expected me to not only be successful in my field but also work to undermine systems of oppression that prevented people like myself from moving forward.

As I thought more about what it meant undermining oppressive systems, I started to recognize that building a dynamic understanding of culture would be necessary for me to effectively do this work. Dr. White had the ability to effortlessly develop relationship with mentees and connect them with the professionals whom they should know. Watching him amplify the importance of relationships, I began to think about Dr. Thomas Parham's Black Psychology class that I attended as an undergraduate student at UC Irvine in 1997. It was there that I was first introduced to the scholarly work of Dr. White. In that class, Dr. Parham helped me to recognize the value of unpacking my thoughts, attitudes, and actions as a Black man. And, though we covered issues related to how Black people have been affected by oppressive forces, he illustrated the possibilities that came from holding on to hope and not allowing oneself to be constrained by societal barriers.

Thinking back to that night in the Los Angeles Marriott, I remember recognizing the importance of the experience. I realize now that it was identity-shaping. I remember feeling like I did not want the intellectual exchange to end. As Dr. White spoke about his experiences and shared his thoughts about how to develop into a leader, I felt as if he was holding a mirror to my soul. As Dr. White continued to "hold court" (i.e., informal mentorship circles), I began to gain insight into the reality that I must give myself permission to succeed and not wait for the validation of our oppressors. I realized that it was my responsibility to find ways to operationalize my skills and vision for leadership. Dr. White mentioned seeing beyond the surface and not "dwell in the average because excellence will bring opportunities." He explained that excellence was valuable, and therefore, it was hard to ignore. And as others shared their stories, I was able to hear about how this philosophy had played out with some of Dr. White's other mentees. I began to understand the importance of distributed expertise and how that was essential to problem-solving.

Looking back, I now understand that meeting with Dr. White created an opportunity for me to learn from a master educator and mentor. He provided me with a template for achieving excellence as I worked to develop myself as an administrative leader in education. I was able to join several emerging educators and psychologists as Dr. White spoke of taking advantage of career opportunities and the importance of goal setting. He explained that it was necessary to align with one's values saying, "Denial will restrict choices and personal growth, interpersonal relationships, and economic opportunities." This began a transformative process for me, shifting my worldview and helping me understand that I needed to be honest with myself about my intentions to thrive. In so many ways, I began to conceptualize what it truly means to put your thoughts into action, even in the most complicated situations. With this in mind, I realized that I needed to define my own strength-based narrative, as if I left myself subject to the constructed realities of others. I could be made invisible and forced to accept the limitations imposed by oppressive stereotypes and bigoted beliefs.

Dr. White said, "Sometimes it only takes a few minutes for you to be your own agent of change. Find the power within and pursue that because excellence will prevail over any level of politics." Moreover, I recall Dr. White quoting the profound words of Ralph Ellison: "When I discover who I am, I will be free." These words reminded me of what W.E.B. Dubois called the "talented tenth" (i.e., the 10% of us who find themselves in leadership positions) and how crucial it was to develop a solid identity to effectively lead. And as the Dr. White's court began to wind down, I began to realize that I would need to be the architect of my life; one decision at a time.

Soon after that evening at the Marriot, I was also invited to attend the Highly Valued Degree Initiative (HVDI) Symposium discussion about the book *Black Fathers: An Invisible Presence in America* (2nd ed.) in Long Beach, California, in February 2013. There was a panel of contributing authors including Dr. White, Dr. Michael E. Connor, Dr. Rashika Rentie, Dr. Lionel Mandy, and Dr. Bedford Palmer II, though Drs. Rentie and Palmer were graduate students at the time. They shared their insights into their chapters and their experiences with Black fathers.

Once the presentations ended, I remember watching Dr. White write a simple note when he signed my copy of the book. It read "Keep the Faith." I remember feeling affirmed and wanting to be more in touch with what makes my work matter. Keeping the faith is taking belief over doubt and staying the course. Also, it is taking the things you are doing to the next level while you are preparing for unknown opportunities. Keeping the faith requires you to believe in the power of your own voice and trust the expertise that you have worked to develop. For me, this meant establishing a foundation to understand myself as a social justice-oriented leader.

Analysis of Narrative

As I think about the wisdom that I was able to glean from Dr. White's word and actions, I realize that a lot of my thinking changed from those interactions. This was a long and difficult process of self-reflection and experimentation. Taking after Dr. White, I have developed my own relationship to fundamental concepts like keeping the faith. For me, this has translated to Holding on with Patient Expectations or HOPE. I found that the seemingly simple act of being honest with myself had life-changing implications. As I witnessed and participated in the "Freedom Train," I realized that it was a revolutionary undertaking and that it must have taken a high level of perseverance, cultural intelligence, honor, humility, and resilience for Dr. White to maintain over the years. Moreover, through the Freedom Train, he provided an alternative space where his mentees were not only able to develop but where they could also receive validation from peers and elders, eschewing the need to seek validation from any oppressor. Within the Freedom Train community, mentees were given the opportunity to experience the highest form of freedom, which is being free from judgment and embraced by positive regard. Getting on the Freedom Train allowed me to work through the changes that inevitably came to my life while taking part in a supportive community.

The term "Keep the faith" resonates with me on many levels. I see it as choosing to stay the course while having the ability to imagine a world that is unseen because we do not consciously recognize our influences. Faith makes us pay close attention to our imagination in ways that can inspire creativity. My faith has helped me to learn how to capture the uncertainty of the moment and to grapple with the ugly truths that can arise. This can especially be the case when circumstances do not align with what you expected. However, I have found that when I was able to recognize the struggle, it provided me with a level of focus that assisted me while I worked toward my goals. Speaking from this perspective, I have found that it was important not shy away from intimidating circumstances, but to instead seek to create opportunities as I worked to become better equipped to look oppression in the face and confront it. Dr. White would often credit much of his growth to his experiences during some of the most challenging times of the civil rights movement in the 1960s. He explained that even while reeling from the pain that he shared with Black communities due to the shock of the assassinations of civil rights and political leaders, and the subsequent civil unrest, even in the midst of unimaginable circumstances, he kept the faith.

I believe that keeping one's faith is the antidote to the fear that dogs leaders who look toward social transformation. As the demand for leaders to take on a more transformative and social justice-oriented lens, future leaders will be forced to engage in a higher degree of critical analysis and activism for social change. It is essential for developing leaders to see this as an opportunity to reject fear-based reactions to engage in proactive inquiry and to break oppressive barriers as they serve their communities. I believe that the ability to address deep concerns with independent thinking allows leaders to overcome some of the barriers that interfere with a full imagining of their potential.

Transformation magnifies vision, insight, and understanding while aligning purposes based on consistency with core beliefs, principles, or values that bring permanent change by applying knowledge, self-perpetuating, and confidence-building (White & Parham, 1990; Covey, 2009; Hill, 2021). I believe that it is important for leaders to be critical of the pressure to adhere to oppressive Eurocentric norms, taking on the stance of a transformational leader. From this perspective, a transformational leader aims to fundamentally change organizations, moving the people and the systems toward a more socially just stance.

Transformational leadership is a leadership approach that causes a change in social systems in individuals and is the process in which leaders and their teams support each other in overall advancement and development (Burns, 1978). Social justice-oriented transformational leadership is collaborative. Self-interest must be put aside to work toward the goals of the communities that you wish to liberate. The structure of transformational teams must allow for a bidirectional transfer of information, enthusiasm, inspiration, and compassion between leaders and their teams. Transformational leaders bring about positive, sustained change in an organization, and the followers are more productive and effective (Bandura, 2001; Leithwood & Sun, 2012). They encourage transparency within organizations, inviting individuals to share their feedback regardless of how it might challenge leadership. Leaders need to be intentional about equity-mindedness and purposely create psychologically safe environments.

Dr. White spoke about the difficulties that occur as one grows in stature as a leader. He explained that progress does not occur in a straight line, and he cautioned that one's goals might be distorted by adherence to Eurocentric norms. Success by any means will likely come at the cost of one's values; yet if you strive to produce excellence, people will notice it. Through this process of fostering excellence, transformational leaders can build prestige and social capital, which can be used in a liberatory fashion to facilitate opportunities for social justice-oriented change.

Practical Strategies

The purpose of the section is to explore best practices in successful leadership. These suggestions are based on my experiences and the lessons I have learned over the course of my career. To elevate the words of Dr. White, "It is vitally important that we develop out of the authentic experience." We must base our decisions on the evidence that we observe in the real world and develop ourselves as leaders to address those observations.

- I have learned that essential aspects of leadership are speaking truth to power/powerless and ensuring that your life backs up your message. Dr. White explained, "Identity congruence outlines the necessary conditions to achieve a purpose or goal." I realized that to be a good leader, I want to know the truth even if it results in conflict.

- You need the wherewithal to be emotionally intelligent, observe, and survey to lead. Desire plays a significant role in anyone's quest to lead because success does not have obligations; it has requirements. There are no shortcuts, and you must do the actual work, meaning that you can overcome obstacles. The requirements can uproot ineffective leaders because they may not have the desire or a caring ambition to become something and pursue excellence. Leading people and overseeing projects will take passion and determination.

- High expectations are a good thing. When mentors share these high expectations, listen for understanding. At times, instructions from mentors do not require an immediate response, but instead the listener should take time to make sense of what is being shared and how they can apply it to their very own situations.

- Big things happen in small places. Building a network that can produce and offer solutions during critical moments is essential. I did not know that a roundtable discussion with Dr. White in a casual setting would be life changing. Career readiness can depend on taking risks and being ready to take advantage of available resources.

- Dr. White said, "future leaders must transform systems that utilize conceptual pitfalls that prevent people from moving towards empowerment." Change is a standard, inevitable, vital, and healthy aspect of leadership. I believe that the inability to take risks impedes transformational processes. We must reframe our understanding of success as a leader, making sure that we prioritize our mission over our image.

- Seek references from people in non-supervisory roles. On my journey toward leadership, I served as a school district administrator, and I gathered recommendations from security guards, instructional aides, and office personnel. Positive relationships with people regardless of hierarchy demonstrate a high level of leadership effectiveness and understanding. It is invaluable to maintain relationships with multiple stakeholder groups to reference your skills and character.

- Communication problems cause conflicts on multiple levels. Increasing communication minimizes pitfalls or failures. Engaging in productive disagreements prevents exhaustion and lethargy from taking effect, as teams want to meet high demands on short deadlines with increasing expectations.

- Morale can be a powerful indicator of organizational health and productivity. Achieving, maintaining, and sustaining employee morale is one of the leadership challenges. In a world fraught with stress-producing events and situations, it isn't easy to maintain a sense of optimism and enthusiasm.

- Responsibility to carry out the mission and vision of the organization must be shared. The cooperative approach emphasizes mutual group goals, understanding others' views, and compromising to develop a mutually useful solution. To be successful, leaders need the skills to manage conflicts, and the approach truly depends on the situation.

Conclusion

The concepts explored in this chapter can serve as a first step in helping future leaders develop an anti-racist perspective as they prepare for leadership to address issues germane to today's changing society. Demanding accountability of systems of oppression can be a hard road to follow. However, recognizing that the journey toward becoming a transformational leader was never meant to be convenient, one must give themselves permission to succeed.

Discussion Questions

1   What are some ways that you engage in critical self-reflection? What are your core values, and how do you cultivate excellence?
2   What kind of barriers impact your access to opportunities? Where are these barriers coming from? What strategies can you use from this chapter to help overcome those barriers?
3   How does your social network create favorable environments for your success? Where are you respected and valued? Where can you be nurtured in your work toward social justice?
4   How do you see yourself in relation to being a socially just leader? What are some traits you would like to develop to be more effective in your leadership?
5   What gives you hope? How do you use hope in order to motivate yourself to push for change?

References

Burns, J. M. (1978). *Leadership*. Harper & Row.

Covey, S. R. (2009). *Principle-centered leadership*. Rosetta Books.

Hill, J. B. (2021). Culture and conversation: Rethinking Brown v. Board of education a postponed commitment to educational equality. *Journal of Education and Learning*, *10*(2), 37–52.

Leithwood, K., & Sun, J. (2012). The nature and effects of transformational school leadership: A meta-analytic review of unpublished research. *Educational Administration Quarterly*, *48*(3), 387–423. https://doi.org/10.1177/0013161X11436268

White, J. L., & Parham, T. A. (1990). *The Psychology of Blacks: An African American Perspective* (2nd Ed). Englewood Cliffs, NJ: Prentice Hall.

12 Excellence as a Pathway to Success

Taisha Caldwell-Harvey

Figure 12.1 Image of Sheetal Shah, Taisha Caldwell-Harvey, Nima Patel, Kathleen Chwalisz, and Joseph L. White (seated). Provided by and used with permission of Taisha Caldwell-Harvey (2022).

Introduction

Dr. White once told me I owed him excellence in response to me insisting on paying a check after a lunch date. I was a broke graduate student and definitely did not have extra cash, but I knew the knowledge he had just imparted on me was worth more than I could ever repay, so I just wanted him to let me pay the check. I imagine now, he must have chuckled to himself on the inside, but he simply looked at

DOI: 10.4324/9781003132899-16

me intensely and said, "just be excellent, that is all you owe." I smiled and agreed politely, but I still felt guilty on the inside. I later learned that guilt was because my understanding of excellence at that time was rooted in a definition constructed by my oppressor. Unbeknownst to me, I would spend a significant amount of my career unpacking and redefining excellence as a means to achieve success. On this journey, I discovered what Dr. White already knew: my excellence truly was the most significant repayment I could ever offer. In this chapter, I redefine success and excellence from a social justice framework and provide practical strategies for utilizing your pursuit of excellence as a means to make strategic career decisions, to identify and create viable growth opportunities, and to be uncompromising about maintaining joy as a critical part of your journey.

Redefining Excellence & Success

According to the dictionary, success is obtaining or achieving wealth, respect, or fame. It is to get the correct or desired outcome of an attempt (Merriam-Webster's Collegiate Dictionary, 2003). By Western standards, the desired result is getting the degree, the job, the house, the car, the life partner, the kids, the dog, and lots of money to buy lots of things (or at least a good amount of money to buy a good amount of things). You get bonus points if you can do all of this by the age of 30 and double bonus points if you also manage to give back a little to those who are less fortunate. No one would argue that a 30-something professional (especially someone from a marginalized community) who had accomplished all of those things wasn't successful.

And as for being excellent? Work hard, give everything you have, win, be the best. That was probably my working definition of excellence if you had asked me right out of college and probably throughout graduate school as well. *Merriam-Webster* agrees and defines excellence as being eminently good, first in class, or superior (Merriam-Webster's Collegiate Dictionary, 2003). Of course, this idea of being excellent was not new to me. As with many Black children, I was taught that I would have to work twice as hard to get half as far in life. I accepted those teachings, and my pursuit of excellence had taken me pretty far. The problem was, I just could not figure out how me, being excellent and becoming successful, as Dr. White insisted, would ever equate to paying him back for the wisdom he shared with me and how he impacted my life (not just during that one lunch but more broadly). I knew that at some point, I would be able to do for others what he had done for me financially, and I already served as a mentor to young girls as a way to give back, but it still did not add up. Why was he so invested? I grappled with accepting his generosity for years and across many mentor sessions. The amount he poured into me and the way I saw him pour into others never entirely made sense. That is until I began to challenge the very definition of success and excellence. It began with me asking myself two questions; who benefits from me working incessantly to achieve wealth, respect, and fame, and what was their ultimate goal? I did not like my answers to those questions as the things I valued, and the people I loved surely were not included as beneficiaries in these Western ideals of how I should live my life. My quest for an alternate perspective led me to the works of W.E.B DuBois, which prompted me to approach these concepts from a social justice lens.

The core principles of social justice require a centering of equity, self-determination, interdependence, and social responsibility in our efforts to ensure the most marginalized in our society have a fair opportunity to live a good life (Adams & Bell, 2016). Thus, from this perspective, success is not about mastering or conquering life; it is about contributing to it, connecting with it, and liberation. Getting all the riches and meeting all the milestones is great, but it is incomplete. To be truly successful, in a way that aligns with social justice in a Western world, the desired outcome of our attempt at life would need to leave us more connected to each other and simultaneously liberated from that which restrains us. Being successful then is the degree to which we can use our unique gifts and talents to advance humanity. Moreover, if we approach the concept of excellence through this same social justice lens, one that again emphasizes self-determination, interdependence, social responsibility, and equity, our definition morphs into one where at its foundation, we matter, our purpose is interconnected, and our joy is a requirement.

We Matter

It seemed Dr. White always traveled in a pack. The first time we met was when he was visiting my graduate university to give a talk. His talk was highly anticipated and was all the buzz around campus for weeks leading up to his arrival. He had a direct mentor relationship with a few of the students in the program, but I had never met him. The first time I saw him, he was walking down a corridor with at least ten other students and faculty surrounding him and talking purposefully. As the group moved directly toward me, I recall thinking, *here is my opportunity to introduce myself!* As he approached, I excitedly said *hello* (so much for trying to stand out). He stopped to acknowledge me and asked my name, where I was from, what program I was in, what I was researching, and maybe one other question before continuing to his destination. It was a brief interaction, but I was pleased to have had the privilege to greet him. I went to his talk that day and attended an evening social where he was an invited guest but did not have any other interaction with him. It was a memorable experience just getting to hear his lecture, meet him briefly, and be among his presence.

However, my second meeting with Dr. White is what will be etched in my mind forever. A year later, I (intentionally) ran into him at a conference. Just as I was trying to figure out how to reintroduce myself and strike up a conversation (I was definitely planning to say more than *hello* this time), he walked directly up to me and with a welcoming and jovial tone exclaimed, "Taisha from San Jose! How you been?" I was shocked. *He knew who I was? He remembered me? How? Why? He remembered my name and where I was from?* After I recovered from my momentary paralysis, we chatted, and he took a few moments to introduce me to several people on the freedom train (his incredible network of professionals) who he thought could support my interests. Dr. White was always facilitating meaningful connections. What I took away from that interaction was that I mattered. Honestly, I never would have even known I did not think I mattered if he had not so clearly demonstrated that I did. The jarring nature of that realization was something of an awakening.

Dr. White was invested in the purpose-driven calling I had on my life, and it mattered to him whether or not I fulfilled it. He wanted me to succeed, and he was willing to use his knowledge, power, and influence to ensure that I did. Our mentor relationship continued to strengthen over the years through a series of brief but intentional interactions. And while I spent little time with him, the impact was profound. It mattered to know he was looking out for me. It mattered that I knew I could call on him if my bravery in pursuit of excellence were ever met with a power to which I could not compete. I never called on him for that, but it emboldened me to do more and to be more. Regardless of whether someone has pointed it out, we all matter.

Our Purpose Is Interconnected

I spent a lot of time figuring out what I wanted to do with my life, and I used to feel frustrated that I was not one of the lucky ones who have known the answer since they were little. Society puts a lot of pressure on us in that way, and it leads many of us to dream up visions of how we want to be. We draw conclusions about how much money we want to make, how much fame we want to have, the size of the home we want to live in, how many children we want to have, how many hours a week we want to work, etc., and then we create a plan to use our gifts to actualize that picture. And all of this makes sense if we are operating with a Western definition of excellence and success where our purpose is to work hard for gain. But when we shift our paradigm to one where we center equity, self-determination, interdependence, and social responsibility, what we are supposed to do with our lives becomes infinitely more significant than what we want for ourselves.

For folks who have a lived experience of being marginalized, sometimes our dreams scare us. The purpose-filled visions that enter our heads can seem big (sometimes huge), and our instinct is often to shut them down and try to think of something else to do because we do not want to be THAT big, or THAT notable, or THAT famous. Then we expend tons of energy trying to make sure our next steps align with the vision we have more practically created for ourselves (the one where we are only medium big). But when we allow ourselves to sit with what it means to move with purpose from a social justice perspective, the reality is that our purpose, what we are supposed to do with our life, is much bigger than any of us individually. We find success through fully developing the unique gifts and talents we were granted and using them to advance humanity.

I suppose we are all fortunate that Dr. White did not decide he did not want to be that big, or that famous, or to be perceived as larger than life. I never saw him try to manage his reputation, but he moved with a calm power that commanded attention whenever he spoke. He was a talented lecturer and storyteller, and from audiences large to small, people could not help but listen with fascination. I do not know if he liked all the attention he received, but I also suppose he figured out that it was not about him somewhere along the way. It was what he was called to do. While we are each given certain gifts for reasons that are not always obvious, when we shift our mindset away from one that says, "being successful is getting what I want," to one where being successful is doing what we are called to do excellently, we are presented with an opportunity to be brave enough to accept whatever responsibility and positioning that come with that.

Our Joy Is a Requirement

There is nothing more amazing than the pure joy you can almost feel in the eyes of a child who is laughing at something really funny. We have access to our full humanity before the world gets ahold of us; we are born with it. It is our birthright. But somewhere between then and starting our journey to build a career, something changes. Life comes at each of us in different ways and can cast a shadow over our naturally joyful spirit. And for those of us who live in a society that does not always affirm our identities, that shadow can feel like a total solar eclipse. Joy then gets so far away from us that it seems like a luxury. And by the time we are a few years into our careers, joy has been redefined as something we can earn if we just work hard enough. We will find joy as soon as we "make it," we tell ourselves. And while this logic seems easy enough to follow, when I think about who benefits from that belief system, hard work without joy is simply a surrendering of my birthright to a system of oppression. Success from a social justice lens requires us to be liberated from that which oppresses us, which means our joy must be built into the now and always. We should not experience less joy simply because of our identities. Our excellence requires joy.

This is not a lesson Dr. White taught directly, but it was always how I saw him. He was never afraid to laugh and enjoy life. I never left a lecture or mentor session without laughing, and I often laughed so hard it hurt. After his speaking engagements, there was always a reception, and you could always count on good wine, good food, and good company. He would boldly recount his experiences navigating great hardships and barrier-breaking, disappointments and failures, racism and disrespect, loss, and all of the hard things that happen to trailblazers. But woven into the seams of every story were tales of joy and comic relief and tidbits about his life and the joy he experienced unapologetically.

This lesson seems simple, but it was the hardest to internalize for me. It required a paradigm shift away from thinking about joy as a self-serving quality that we earn to one where joy is simply a requirement for each of us to have access to all we are meant to be. It is something we simply need to move purposefully through life. I felt this most clearly at his death. I felt a deep sadness, but surprisingly, I also felt a sense of joy and gratefulness at the same time. His life was a testament to our hearts' capacity to hold joy through any circumstance.

Summary

In a world where we matter, our purpose is interconnected, and our joy is a requirement, the formula to remember is that excellence = hard work in pursuit of purpose + joy. A lot of people are just out here doing stuff and getting stuff. They set goals and check seemingly impressive tasks off their never-ending to-do lists. But at the end of each day, month, and year, many of those people will still be unfulfilled. I would argue this is because most of us do not want to just do stuff; we want to do stuff that matters. We want to be a version of success that leaves us liberated from our oppressor. Being truly excellent is your most direct path to that type of success.

Dr. White did not buy me lunch all those years ago and mentor me because he liked me. He was inspiring a generation. He was living excellently by doing what he was called to do. So, me having the resources and guidance (and nourishment) to do what I was supposed to do was inextricably tied to his success and vice versa. He knew that, and now so do I.

Practical Strategies for Utilizing Your Pursuit of Excellence as a Means to Success

Utilizing these decolonized definitions, I share my best advice and road map to being successful as you navigate oppressive spaces, find your voice, connect to your purpose, and develop influence.

1 **Accept your purpose and divine calling to greatness even if you don't know what it is.**

Following the wisdom of an African proverb, from the moment you took your first breath, you had purpose. Your life had meaning, and you were given unique gifts to nurture. Those gifts will usher you into the fullest expression of all you were meant to be when nurtured in the proper contexts. Trust in this truth even if life has taken you on a whirlwind journey, and you have no idea where you landed. By the time we are eight months old, we develop object permanence. It is our ability to know that something exists even if we cannot see it. Just because you can't see your purpose doesn't mean it doesn't exist. It exists, and it matters that you find it, align yourself with it, and fulfill it. Our minds are powerful and can either propel our wildest dreams or keep us stuck behind an imaginary wall of blocked possibility. Don't allow the lies of your oppressor to trick you into believing that who you are and what you are meant to do is small or insignificant. The impact you are meant to make is infinite. Seek it through exploration.

2 **Seek purpose through exploration.**

Right after I graduated with my doctoral degree, I had a meltdown while talking with another of my mentors (who also happens to be a direct mentee of Dr. White). Completing my degree was a huge accomplishment, but truth be told, after all the dust settled, it felt very anticlimactic. Suddenly, the thing I had worked so hard toward was here, and I had no idea what was next. I kept asking myself, *what am I supposed to do now?*

In discussing the next steps with my mentor, he told me to follow my North Star. It is a concept he mentioned often, and while it never made much sense to me, I never questioned it. However, as he repeated it on this particular day, while I was feeling extremely frustrated, I just returned a blank stare as tears started welling up in my eyes. I was overwhelmed by the pressure to have it all figured out, to plan for my next move, and to do it fast because time was ticking! In a slightly more aggressive tone than I intended, and just as the tears started to pour down my face, I blurted out, "I don't know what I'm doing! I don't have a North Star! The sky is dark!" In case you ever find yourself in this position, feeling without direction, I will summarize the advice he gave me.

You are not lost; you are searching. The ability to spend time seeking purpose is a gift. Give yourself permission to live in exploration without the fear of time running out. These moments in between periods of grinds offer you time for rest and reflection. Cherish this part of your journey, and come to appreciate these moments. Your goal during these times is simply to explore. Align your decisions with actions that will help you expand your thinking and offer you new experiences. Trust that within this process, your North Star will shine again. And just like that, I had a plan, and now so do you!

3   **Make a lifelong commitment to the mastery of your craft.**

In a world where anyone can sell a dream with a pretty picture on social media, remember that smoke and mirrors will always just be smoke and mirrors. Your ability to fully utilize your unique gifts and talents relies on your commitment to mastering your craft. The secret sauce of the freedom train is that everyone is good at what they do. The admission price is a commitment to upholding the reputation of high-quality output and always acting with integrity. You do not have to be perfect (perfect does not exist), but you do need to be good at what you say you do. So, find what you are good at and master it. Never stop learning, never stop growing, never stop nurturing your gifts.

4   **Make good career decisions**.

People are drawn to excellence like bees to honey. As you become more successful and exude more and more excellence, opportunities will start to flow. At certain points in your life, it will feel overwhelming, and you will start having to make decisions about what opportunities to capitalize on and what opportunities to pass on. Imagine having to decide between accepting a prestigious fellowship position or writing a column for *Oprah Magazine*, or between two jobs that seemingly would pull you down opposite career paths, or between accepting a board seat and starting your own business. These crossroads are inevitable, and there is a secret to making them easier. Make good decisions, and avoid bad ones.

Simply put, a good decision brings you closer to your ultimate goal and purpose, and a bad decision veers you further away. Reflect on your purpose, noting what impact you are meant to have on the world. Then ask yourself if each decision brings you closer to that or veers you away. Always choose the things that are in alignment with your purpose. This process will allow you to separate beautiful distractions from purposeful movement.

5   **Reach all around you. Up down, left right**.

One of the biggest lies of the oppressor is to trick you into believing that resources are limited and that you become successful by doing it all on your own. The reality is that your oppressor is the only one who benefits from you struggling in isolation and competing for resources. Recall that success, from a social justice perspective, is not about mastering or conquering life. It is about contributing to it, connecting with it, and seeking liberation. In your pursuit of success, make sure to reach up, reach down, reach left and right. Remind yourself daily that there is room for all of our excellence. Help people, collaborate, mastermind with people, and seek mentorship. *Ubuntu* is a South African saying that means *I am because we are.* So, if you are because we are, helping the collective "we" helps you. The greater we are collectively, the greater you are individually. Never stop reaching in all directions as you climb.

6 **Be radical in your commitment to joy at every step.**

Excellence requires joy, joy leads to happiness, and happiness unlocks the depths of your brilliance. Contrary to common belief, there is no magic endpoint where happiness just shows up, and it is not something that you will earn by reaching milestones. Happiness does not come because you got the job, completed the degree, or earned a certain income. People do not tell you that success does not usually feel like the fantasy portrayed in the media. It is messy and has ups and downs, and it includes moments of confusion and self-doubt and soul searching and discovery. But even in the midst of all of that, you can still find happiness. Happiness comes from the cumulative impact of the moments of joy you experience during your life. Sometimes those moments of joy find you, but mostly, you have to create them intentionally.

Imagine starting law school and making sure to schedule monthly day trips with your closest friends throughout the entirety of your first year. Imagine going through a breakup but making sure to take your cousin up on their offer to watch clips of your favorite comedian each week over video chat because it always makes you laugh hysterically. Imagine celebrating with a fancy dinner every time you book a speaking engagement or lead a jaw-dropping presentation. Imagine making celebrating you the norm and being intentional about initiating a small moment of joy every single day of your life. Success is not an endpoint. It is what happens to you on the journey. Your journey will be more meaningful when you choose to be radical about your commitment to joy. This is something you can do right now, and it feels incredible.

Discussion Questions

1 What definitions of excellence and success have you been operating under? Who benefits from it, and what is their ultimate goal?

2 Who matters to you, and how would they know? How can you be more intentional about demonstrating that others matter to you through your behavior? What is one way you can communicate that someone matters with only five minutes of your time?

3 Make a list of your community of support. Who are the people ahead of you, beside you, and behind you? How can you grow and strengthen these relationships?

4 How is your success connected to the success of others? How have you been supportive?

5 Since joy is required for you to have full access to your unique gifts and talents, what are three behaviors you can commit to so that you can experience joy daily?

References

Adams, M., & Bell, L. A. (2016). Theoretical foundations for social justice education. In M. Adams and L. A. Bell (Eds.) *Teaching for diversity and social justice* (pp. 21–44). Routledge.

Martín-Baró, I. (1994). The Psychology of Politics and the Politics of Psychology. In A. Aron and S. Corne, (Eds.) *Writings for a liberation psychology.* Harvard University Press.

Merriam-Webster. (2003). *Merriam-Webster's collegiate dictionary* (11th ed.).

Index

Note: *Italic* page numbers refer to figures and page numbers followed by "n" denote endnotes.

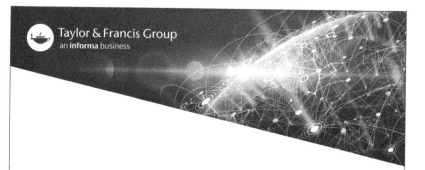